Australian Department Heads Under Howard: Career Paths and Practice

Collected Articles from *The Canberra Times*

Australian Department Heads Under Howard: Career Paths and Practice

Collected Articles from *The Canberra Times*

Paul Malone

THE AUSTRALIAN NATIONAL UNIVERSITY

E PRESS

The Canberra Times

ANU

E PRESS

the Australia and New Zealand
School of Government

Published by ANU E Press
The Australian National University
Canberra ACT 0200, Australia
Email: anuepress@anu.edu.au
Web: http://epress.anu.edu.au

National Library of Australia
Cataloguing-in-Publication entry

Malone, Paul, 1947- .
Australian department heads under Howard : career paths and
practice.

Bibliography.
ISBN 1 920942 82 3 (pbk.)
ISBN 1 920942 83 1 (online)

1. Civil service - Australia - Officials and employees. 2.
Civil service - Australia. 3. Australia - Officials and
employees - Biography. 4. Australia - Politics and
government - 1996- . I. Title.

352.2930994

Cover design by John Butcher

The chapters in this monograph are based on a series of articles originally published in
The Canberra Times between 14 November 2005 and 22 April 2006.

Funding for this monograph series has been provided by the Australia and New
Zealand School of Government Research Program.

John Wanna, *Series Editor*

Professor John Wanna is the Sir John Bunting Chair of Public Administration at the Research School of Social Sciences at The Australian National University. He is the director of research for the Australian and New Zealand School of Government (ANZSOG). He is also a joint appointment with the Department of Politics and Public Policy at Griffith University and a principal researcher with two research centres: the Governance and Public Policy Research Centre and the nationally-funded Key Centre in Ethics, Law, Justice and Governance at Griffith University. Professor Wanna has produced around 17 books including two national text books on policy and public management. He has produced a number of research-based studies on budgeting and financial management including: *Budgetary Management and Control* (1990); *Managing Public Expenditure* (2000), *From Accounting to Accountability* (2001) and, most recently, *Controlling Public Expenditure* (2003). He has just completed a study of state level leadership covering all the state and territory leaders — entitled *Yes Premier: Labor leadership in Australia's states and territories* — and has edited a book on Westminster Legacies in Asia and the Pacific — *Westminster Legacies: Democracy and responsible government in Asia and the Pacific*. He was a chief investigator in a major Australian Research Council funded study of the Future of Governance in Australia (1999-2001) involving Griffith and the ANU. His research interests include Australian and comparative politics, public expenditure and budgeting, and government-business relations. He also writes on Australian politics in newspapers such as *The Australian*, *Courier-Mail* and *Canberra Times* and has been a regular state political commentator on ABC radio and TV.

Table of Contents

Foreword

It is a noteworthy indicator of change in a public service that it is now possible for a journalist, with official sanction, to write profiles of departmental secretaries based on interviews. Until the mid-1960s department heads were rarely mentioned in the media. An attempt in the immediate post-Menzies era to profile secretaries ended in grief after only two interviews.

In the end, the attempt was not entirely futile for, in subsequent years, journalists became adept in covering bureaucracy. In Australia, *the Canberra Times* led the way with a succession of highly skilled reporters on the *public service round*. The unlikely pathfinder was the irascible Bruce Juddery. The first great story revolved around the controversy over use of the VIP flight in the RAAF during the last months of the Holt Government. It was followed hard apace by newly-installed Prime Minister John Gorton's removal, early in 1968, of Sir John Bunting from the post of Secretary, Prime Minister's Department. The *round* was rewarded with especially rich pickings in the days of the McMahon Government and the temperamental, erratic Whitlam prime ministership.

The baton is now in the hands of Paul Malone, author of this monograph. Malone is very well equipped for this assignment. His career in journalism includes 12 years working in the Press Gallery (five as political correspondent and bureau chief for *the Canberra Times*, the rest for the *Financial Review* and the *Sydney Morning Herald*). He has also seen bureaucracy from the inside, as a departmental officer and as a ministerial staffer.

These profiles show that while most of those who reach to top of the public service come from the career service, it is now probable that they will have had a range of experience elsewhere, often in a university, very occasionally in commerce. This experience might come at the start of a career or during a short break after some advancement up the ladder.

In many respects the secretary cadre is very diverse; at around 20 in number it can hardly hope to be representative of the entire nation. They come from all states and Territories, except Tasmania and the Northern Territory, with Victoria predominating, and from abroad. For Peter Shergold, arriving in Australia in his 20s, the route to Secretary, Department of the Prime Minister and Cabinet, was probably more assured than had he entered Whitehall, aspiring to head the British Cabinet Office. Three of the group covered in this book have had no post in Australian Government except as departmental secretaries. All have university qualifications, gained, with one exception, full-time. Most have second degrees, in five cases at doctoral level.

A number have combined experience in Canberra with periods abroad, usually but not entirely in Western Europe or North America, or both. Apart from the three recruited directly as department secretaries, public service experience in Australia outside Canberra is unusual but not entirely absent. Regional experience is obviously not obligatory in the climb to the top.

For a public service based on merit, the collective portrait contained in this book will be reassuring. But it should not be entirely so. It is replete with many views, especially on work-life balance, which will be well-received and perceived as progressive. But there are other matters which show that, beyond the jargon, older bureaucratic instincts and insecurities are far from absent, though sometimes with good reason.

In his introduction, Paul Malone comments on the preponderance of training in economics among the secretaries and revives the debate about economic rationalism promoted a decade or so ago by sociologist Michael Pusey. It is not surprising that economics training should figure so prominently. Walter Bagehot described economics as the "science of business". It is also a "science of government". It is a logical course of study for someone wanting a career in government; and it is not surprising that people with training in economics should subsequently seek a career in government service.

Malone worries that so restricted a disciplinary background could too easily lead to "group think" within government. There are indeed disturbing signs of "group think" in the profiles, but its source does not necessarily lie in disciplinary background.

If anything, the secretaries protest too much about the collegiality and cooperativeness of their whole-of-government endeavours in contrast to what they see as great turf wars of earlier generations. They may be right that the environment has changed, and Malone may be partly right in attributing it to encroaching disciplinary homogeneity, but other explanations are possible. The post-1987 departmental machinery of government structure, based on comprehensive, rather than specialist, departments is a key conditioning factor. It ranks as one of the most significant administrative changes in the Commonwealth during the late twentieth century.

Effective eviction of posts previously held by engineers and other specialists has removed some tough, dogmatic participants from policy debates at the highest levels. Sol Trujillo, at Telstra, is their heir. Furthermore, the great debates which marked the Keynesian era have been settled, largely in favour of economists, certainly insofar as government intervention in (as opposed to regulation of) the economy and the scale and scope of the welfare state are concerned.

This monograph is always interesting and, for anyone seeking to gain a feel for the character and nature of life at the top, it is well recommended. It raises plenty of issues for discussion – sometimes by its virtual silence – from politicisation and accountability to management and staff relations.

J. R. Nethercote
Canberra, Australia
September 2006

Preface

The articles in this collection were first published in *the Canberra Times* between 14 November 2005 and 22 April 2006 in a slightly different format. In some cases two articles were published on the one secretary. These have been combined into one and minor edits and corrections have been made. The articles have not been updated to take account of events since they were first published.

The series aimed to provide a personal profile of the Commonwealth portfolio secretaries, their rise through the service and the challenges their departments faced.

Heads of departments have little to gain by stepping into the limelight and many are wary of the media. From the outset it was agreed that they would not be grilled on current political events. It was my hope that they would provide some inside information on historic events and some insight into policy development and program deliver. In the upshot many readily told fascinating tales of their experiences in administration during major political developments.

This series was only made possible because of the support of Dr Peter Shergold, Secretary of the Department of the Prime Minister and Cabinet, who put my proposal to a portfolio secretaries meeting. Some secretaries initially expressed a reluctance to participate but in the end all agreed. I would like to thank Dr Shergold and the secretaries for their co-operation.

In closing, I would also like to thank John Butcher, John Nethercote and John Wanna for their assistance in preparing this manuscript.

Paul Malone
September 2006

Introduction

If you are a student with ambitions to reach the top in the Australian public service and today's department heads are any guide, there is no question about what subject you should be studying – economics. Thirty or more years ago a good general education might have done. Former lawyers, doctors, scientists or even teachers could be found in numbers in chief executive positions in the key portfolio departments. Today they are a rarity.

It is no surprise to find that the heads of Treasury, or the departments of Finance, or Industry Tourism and Resources are economists. But when one realises that the chief executives of the departments of Heritage and Environment, Agriculture, Fisheries and Forestry, Human Services and Veterans' Affairs are also economists one starts to wonder whether things have gone a little too far. This concern is heightened when it emerges that the head of the Department of the Prime Minister and Cabinet is an economic historian, the head of Communications Information Technology and the Arts has a family background in economics and the key part of her early career was in Treasury/Finance, and the head of Transport and Regional Development developed an early interest in economics and completed a diploma in the subject.

Contrast this with the bureaucracy in 1970. Defence was headed by Sir Henry Bland, a lawyer; Civil Aviation by Sir Donald Anderson, ex RAAF and a teacher; Education and Science by Sir Hugh Ennor, a biochemist; and Repatriation by Brigadier Sir Frederich Chilton, a lawyer/soldier. The Prime Minister's Department, External Affairs and the Treasury were headed by commerce or economics graduates as was Trade and Industry, but at Trade the economist, Sir Alan Westerman, was ready, willing and able to challenge Treasury views and often refused to sing the Treasury song.

The trend in economists dominating the public service was identified by Michael Pusey in his 1991 book, *Economic Rationalism in Canberra*. Pusey found that of 215 senior executive service officers in the key departments, 44 per cent had degrees in economics or commerce, or designated themselves as economists. He also found that those with an economics cum business background were more conservative than their counterparts with degrees in the other social sciences and humanities.

From the top 18 department heads I interviewed, I cannot say whether the economists are more or less conservative than the others. But the danger is that we have developed a like-minded class of politicians and senior bureaucrats. A time lag naturally occurs between the recruitment of staff and their promotion to the top jobs. Retired soldiers, sailors and air force men, recruited after 1945, dominated the service in the 1960s and 1970s. Today's department heads were the middle ranking officers of 15 to 20 years ago when the dominant issues were economic.

The service was also significantly larger and different in composition in the post-war years with departments such as Postmaster-Generals, Works and Supply employing many people and directly involved in delivering services and building infrastructure.

In his 2004 Sir Roland Wilson lecture, the Head of the Department of the Prime Minister and Cabinet, Dr Peter Shergold, said there was a tendency to look back on the secretaries of the past with nostalgia, finding in them qualities which reflected badly on the contemporary incumbents. Shergold argued that today's public service leadership is subject to greater scrutiny than in the past and that the occasional failure of the public service did not indicate a conspiracy of politicisation. He maintained that the service should be more responsive to the Government of the day.

Shergold was responding to media criticism of the subservience of the service. Some of the criticism may have been unfair but there were also well informed internal critics of the direction in which the service had moved. A year earlier the Public Service Commissioner, Andrew Podger had pointed out that prime ministers Whitlam, Fraser, Hawke, Keating and Howard had all felt that the service was too slow to respond to their democratically determined authority. But he said the sustained increase in emphasis on responsiveness "must have increased the risk to our other obligations of being apolitical and openly accountable, as there is inevitably some tension between these obligations." He added, "We would be silly to deny this." On his retirement in 2005, Podger, who interestingly is a science honours graduate, repeated much the same comments.

Shergold maintains that the secretarial responsibility is well set out in the *Public Service Act* where it states that, "The APS is responsive to the Government in providing frank, honest, comprehensive, accurate and timely advice and in implementing the Government's policies and programs." Shergold asserts that it is not sufficient for Sercretaries to be frank and fearless in standing up to their ministers - equally important, and fundamental to their role, is that their advice be "responsive to the directions set by government and committed to the effective delivery of policy decisions taken by government." He said it was the Government alone which decided on national interest.

Today every senior bureaucrat hails whole-of-government policy development and program delivery. He, or she, can't get enough of co-operative and collegiate approaches. They will all assure you that they are nevertheless able to give frank and fearless advice. But the danger is that coming from such similar educational and cultural backgrounds, a group-think mentality, combined with an enthusiasm for co-operation, produces homogeneous policy.

All secretaries say, of course, that they welcome a variety of views. By the nature of government, alternative internal views are not publicised and policy paper leaks, revealing strongly opposing views, are rare. But what if there is a need to challenge? Take the decision to commit Australian troops to the Iraq war, for example. Public opposition to the war was strong and there were many well informed outsiders able to put a strong case against participation. But we have no evidence that such a case was argued internally. The publicly available evidence suggests that the key departments and agencies meekly took up the Prime Minister's intention to take Australia to war and managed the process on his behalf. A public servant who might disagree, such as Andrew Wilkie, had little option but to resign.

Similarly in Immigration the senior levels of the bureaucracy and the department itself took up with the anti-asylum-seeker populist culture that the Government found politically marketable in the late 1990s and earlier this decade. Today the head of Immigration, Andrew Metcalfe, who was brought in to reshape the department after the Rau and Solon deportation and detention debacles, but who also had a long association with the department in the period when the poor culture developed, says that clearly the department got some things very wrong.

He says that between 1999 and 2002 he had a strong sense of an organisation often in crisis management mode but he did not have a sense of the culture being wrong to the extent that events had since shown. Were there any internal voices challenging the culture? Despite the codes of practice which should enable staff to speak up, there is no public evidence to suggest there were dissenting internal voices.

The heads of the departments of Environment and Heritage and Agriculture, Fisheries and Forestry both proudly point to the co-operative relationship now employed to look after land and water management. This arrangement − developed by their economics-qualified predecessors, Roger Beale and Mike Taylor − followed years of acrimonious relationships in the late 1980s when the departments and their ministers were at loggerheads. Today Environment is headed by an economist, David Borthwick and DAFF is headed by another economist, Joanna Hewitt. This small fact does not mean that they must see every issues as economists might. Nor does it mean that they demand an economist's perspective from their department. But one cannot help wondering if, for example, a scientist trained in environmental issues might set the agenda for the Environment department in a slightly different way and whether this might produce a less cosy, but more beneficial outcome for Australia.

One might also ask if in the Department of Employment and Workplace Relations today there is genuine research going on to determine whether the new Workplace Relations legislation might create a new class of working poor in

Australia. And if a researcher were to reach such a conclusion would it be published?

One mantra that everyone in the service sings is the need to cut red tape. But this has not stopped the passage of 1000 pages of Workplace Relations legislation and the 400 pages of regulations that go with it.

While the Secretaries may have an over-representation of economists, their family backgrounds are more varied than one might expect. One surprising discovery was how many come from a non-urban background. Dr Ken Henry, head of Treasury is the son of a North Coast timber logger; Dr Peter Boxall, the head of the Department of Employment and Workplace Relations, grew up on a small farm in Victoria; Joanna Hewitt, head of Agriculture Fisheries and Forestry, is the daughter of a bank manager but lived in nearly every little town in Western Australia attending eight or nine rural schools; Mike Taylor, at Transport and Regional Services, claims a mixed upbringing in urban and rural Victoria; Andrew Metcalfe, head of Immigration grew up in Toowoomba; and even the Canberra identity, Jane Halton, the head of Health and Ageing, spent her primary years in a small English country village.

One possible explanation for the larger than expected number of people from country backgrounds at the top of the service is that it is a meritocracy, providing an opportunity for people without connections to gain promotion. The smaller number of *old-school-tie* bureaucrats today might also be explained by their shift to the more lucrative private sector, leaving government and Catholic school graduates to struggle up the service ladder.

One change which has occurred over the last couple of years to make the top echelons of the service more representative of the population is the appointment of some women to high level positions. Five of the top 18 are now women, not yet pro rata, but moving in the right direction and certainly a dramatic improvement from the 1970s and 1980s. Helen Williams at Communications, the longest serving secretary, was a pioneer in this battle. But most of the other women had stories of blatant discrimination to tell in their rise through the ranks. It might be expected that these women bring an added perspective to policy development and contribute to a more balanced approach.

But what of ethnic diversity at the top of the service? Despite all the southern and eastern European migration since the 1950s, and the migration from all over the world in more recent year, there is not one Pappadopoulous, Spasojevic, Wong or Singh at the top. A near compulsory part of every job interview in the service is adherence to the principles of equal opportunity and diversity but this has not permeated all the way up.

Anecdotal comments suggest that this may well be due to the fact that a certain type of behaviour and style is expected in the service, one that fits neither the flamboyant southern European, nor the more restrained Asian. The people at the top select people like themselves, albeit with some men now willing to select like-minded and (similar personality type) women. In recent years, for a whole variety of reasons, indigenous representation has fallen at all levels in the service and there is currently no indigenous person in the wings of the service, ready for a top job.

An "exotic" at the top in the service is someone like Dr Peter Shergold. Shergold is unusual for a number of reasons: a British migrant, a late recruit to the service and an economic historian, rather than full blooded economist (there is a difference – economic historians tend to know more about the real world). Lisa Paul, head of Education, Science and Training, and Jane Halton have some claim to being exotic. Not only are they women but they were both were born overseas – Paul in the United States and Halton in Britain.

In his 1991 book Pusey found that even twenty years after leaving school, family background had an influence on the disposition of senior public servants. Today the elite private school does not seem to have quite the influence it once had. Michael L'Estrange at the Department of Foreign Affairs and Trade stands out for his attendance at the exclusive Catholic, St Aloysius College, Milson's Point.

A mandatory qualification for appointment to a chief executive position is of course a stint at one of the central agencies, Prime Minister and Cabinet, Treasury or Finance. This increases the chances that an economist will come to the notice of the Prime Minister and become a candidate for a top job. But with the recent increase in emphasis on security, and the creation of more advisory positions in that field, it would not be surprising to find that in a few years more people with a background in this area will take CEO positions.

This article was first published in the Canberra Times on 22 April 2006

The Consummate 'Fixer' – Peter Shergold, Department of the Prime Minister and Cabinet

Dr Peter Shergold has not always looked forward to coming into work. For those who know him as the upbeat, bouncy, optimistic head of the Department of the Prime Minister and Cabinet, this may seem surprising. Nothing seems to get Shergold down now. He thrives on the pressure of work as Australia's most senior public servant. It is no hardship coming in at 8 am and leaving at 7.30 pm five days a week and dropping into the office to clear the desk of all paperwork on Sunday morning. The relentless hard work is overcome by the fact that, "it's thoroughly exciting, absorbing, interesting work", he says. He may not like the lack of autonomy over his time but he is happy to pay this price.

It was not always so. Eleven years ago, in his final six months as CEO of the Aboriginal and Torres Strait Islander Commission, he says he was "not looking forward every morning to going to work … I had done three years by then and it was relentlessly difficult. And it is sometimes difficult to keep your spirits up … Sometimes when people say it must be tough being head of PM&C, or it must have been tough when you were working in DEWR during the waterfront dispute, I disagree. I always think that if you've done three and a half years trying to administer aboriginal affairs, you can take anything – it is a genuinely difficult area. You know that people's lives depend upon it … It's a very emotionally fraught area and it is certainly a great school for toughening you up."

Shergold's time at ATSIC may in the end have been morale sapping. But at its conclusion his minister, Robert Tickner, said he had "played a simply magnificent role." Nevertheless a major career setback followed. "When my contract ended the only position that was found for me was as the head of Comcare", he says. "Now that was a demotion, because it was back to a deputy secretary level and of course it was an area in which I had almost zero expertise. I suppose the thing I learned from that was that any area, if you throw yourself into it, can be a great learning opportunity … I learnt about occupational health and safety. I learnt about actuarialism. I learnt about management and the way that management can influence the rate of stress related illnesses and occupational overuse syndrome … Now I suppose it would have been very easy to have been bitterly disappointed. That having done a pretty tough two and a half years as CEO of ATSIC at the end of it, I was relegated back to a deputy secretary position, which was my substantive level…What I learned from that is that if you persevere, if you take what opportunities come to you and do the job the best you can, that new opportunities come around."

Shergold's background and career path is not one that would be expected to lead to the top job in the Australian Public Service. Firstly, he has not spent his whole career in the public service. As a student in Hull, he had ambitions to be a poet, but turned to economic history. In 1971 he was appointed lecturer in economics at the University of New South Wales and stayed in academia until 1987, when he took his first public service job as head of the Office of Multicultural Affairs. He then spent time in eight more agencies delivering programs in social services areas before getting the top job.

This route to the top was dramatically different to many of his predecessors who mostly followed central agency tracks. But his experiences created a man for his times. The major economic changes that were shepherded through the 1980s, 1990s and early this century of floating the exchange rate, cutting tariffs, deregulating the banks, privatising public enterprises and introducing a goods and services tax, have given way to a host of social policy and security issues. Shergold nominates workplace relations, vocational education, welfare to work and new approaches to indigenous affairs as areas that have become central to the Government's policy agenda and which coincide with areas in which he has had a lot of experience. "I've been lucky in coming to head this department at a time when those issues have been very much at the forefront of the Government's agenda", he says. "I've obviously had to learn a great deal in terms of international diplomacy, security, counter-terrorism, defence because I had no background in those areas."

On the economic side, because of his academic background, he is more comfortable with the issues. His strong focus on program delivery over policy development reflects his work experience, although he sees the two going hand in hand. "I think it's vital in looking at policy development to take account of the experience of the people who are actually delivering the programs because I've seen that for myself", he says. He also believes that Government policy needs to be looked at from outside the Canberra perspective and takes his role of public service leadership very seriously. This, he says, comes from having had experience as Public Service Commissioner.

If there is one area where he has strongly entered the public arena it is in the debate over the willingness of public servants to give frank and fearless advice to ministers. He rejects any suggestion of a golden era in the past, when public servants were more courageous than they are today and adds that he thinks people over-estimate the courage required to give policy advice. "I don't find that it requires a great deal, particularly when you're giving it in private", he says. But he points to times when his administrative responsibilities required some courage. Working on the Job Network tender process, for example, he found that the key public provider, Employment National, had done very badly in the tender process. This presented enormous problems for the Government, particularly as it would result in a significant decline in staff in this public sector organisation.

"Now I have to say that it took some resolve to say to ministers, 'this is the result of the tender which I intend to sign off on and it's going to be a real problem for the Government because you're going to have to deal with the situation in which large numbers of public servants are going to lose their jobs. I apologise but, for probity reasons, this must be my responsibility'. The ministers accepted that ... Now I think that takes courage because unlike policy advice – and on occasion I argue strongly for a piece of policy advice – I fully accept that at the end of the day, it's the Prime Minister, or the Cabinet, that makes the final decision. Not myself."

Shergold is by far the most publicly accessible head of the Prime Minister's department. His predecessor Max Moore-Wilton – now head of Sydney Airport Corporation – was well known by reputation but hid behind bureaucratic walls. His public speeches were few and far between and media interviews were rare. Shergold delivers regular speeches setting out the public service's role and defending the service, and he is open to questioning. "I feel that one of my key jobs is to try and ... act as a facilitator between stakeholders and government", he says. "I think it is entirely appropriate that a whole range of people in the community share my interest in public policy. It is appropriate that I can talk to them about the directions of the public service, talk about the directions that the Government is setting, answer questions and seek their views ... I try as much as I can to be publicly available ... It's tricky because there is the constant risk that in an unguarded moment, I might say something off the cuff which could be used to attack the Government or the Prime Minister. And therefore I am wary but I believe it is better to do it – to try and manage those risks than to not deal with people directly."

Shergold acknowledges he has made mistakes "and you learn from them." He says, for example, that he discovered only under questioning at Senate Estimates that there was evidence that a large Job Network provider had been inappropriately taking fees for job placements. He had not been aware that this was happening and he moved quickly to have a full investigation and resolve the matter. Today he says the thing he is most proud of is the way he has been able to build around him an extraordinarily active intelligent and collegiate group of secretaries. They have to a very considerable extent embraced the idea of working together and he thought departments worked together much more closely than in the past. He believes he is creating a new culture of people working across bureaucratic demarcations. For this reason he strongly supports the notion of a single senior executive service.

Shergold says he sees the role of PM&C as making sure that the Prime Minister, when he chairs Cabinet or COAG meetings, is well placed to be able to get the best outcome on behalf of the Commonwealth Government. "That means making sure that the Prime Minister is very well briefed and that the submissions that come forward from other ministers have answered all the key questions and make it clear what the purpose of the new policy is … [It means making sure] we have consulted appropriately and that agencies have an effective implementation plan…Now the reality is I don't think a department like PM&C can simply co-ordinate, because that suggests that all the department does is simply react to things. In my view the department has to be pro-active. I think the department should be putting forward possible new policy approaches to the Prime Minister … It doesn't mean we go out and second guess every policy. But there are certain issues on which the Prime Minister would like to see the department give clear directions or even, perhaps for the short term, take a leadership role."

He says PM&C "can take a leadership role by chairing an Inter-Departmental Committee (IDC) or hosting a taskforce. On some key issues like vocational education, water policy or energy policy, the department can help the Prime Minister drive a reform process, particularly at the early stages before responsibility goes back to the line agency. These tended to be areas where responsibility did not neatly sit with a particular agency. This could help moderate departmental demarcation disputes and could help things happen quickly…Now there is a danger … that because PM&C … has the power that comes from being the gateway into Cabinet, there is a possibility that that can be misused or can be perceived to be misused … There is a danger in PM&C being seen to be the regulator, the policeman, the second guesser. I don't want to suggest that we've got it completely right because, as always, mistakes get made. But certainly the management ethos I try to drive, the key message I get out every month when I talk to new employees coming into the department … is that I do not want PM&C to be achieving its objects through the use of power and force … That may be successful in the short term. It is not successful in the medium to long term."

This article was first published in the Canberra Times on 14 November 2005

From Timber to Tax – Ken Henry, The Treasury

When Ken Henry was 13, his father, a timber worker cutting logs out of the Landsdowne State Forest near Taree, in the mid North Coast of NSW, came home excited and early and bundled his boys into his car. Normally he'd leave before sun-up and be home after sundown, but this afternoon he took the three brothers down to the sawmill. "He wanted to show us the log he'd taken out of the forest that day", Henry says. "The thing was huge. He was a short man. He stood at the base of the log and it just towered over him. It must have been two metres in diameter. It was as big a log as the biggest log truck could carry, just one log. That's all that would fit on it. You see these log trucks rattling round the ACT and they might have 30 pine trees on them. This was one log and when I spoke to him subsequently about it he said the truck was probably overweight. He also told me that he had had to climb a long way up the tree to get to a point where he could remove this log himself because he was just one man with one chainsaw. Well we started asking questions like how old was the tree the log had come from? He told us anywhere between 100 and 500 years old."

"How many houses could you build with that log? He said 'the framing for three pretty good sized houses'. 'Whoa, it must be worth a lot. Well, dad, how much do you get paid?' 'A few dollars'. 'So who gets the rest of the money? Does the sawmill get the rest?' And he said, and this was very revealing to me, he said, 'Oh No. No. The State Government takes some money as well in royalties, like a tax'. I said, 'Ok fair enough. How much?' He said there'd be a few dollars royalty. And the penny dropped. Like 'hang on, this tree has been in Australia longer than white settlement … it can properly be regarded as the property of the people of NSW. And the Government of NSW had effectively sold it off to a sawmill operator for a few dollars'. That had a profound impact."

So what does this tell Henry today? "It teaches you that governments have responsibilities, including responsibilities over the assets of the people that they represent – timber stocks, fish stocks, quality of the air, water, generally the quality of the environment. When you see something that grates or offends, where you think the outcome is inequitable, where somebody's getting away with something they shouldn't be getting away with, there's a temptation for people to point the finger at the operation of markets and say, 'well, that's how the free market operates, right?' There's a temptation to say 'well, it's all the fault of the free market'. But often it's not. More often than not it's poor government policy."

As an economist Henry agrees that markets handle assets by setting a price and adds that, "nobody ever asked the people of NSW at what price they would be prepared to sell that tree." Well, at what price should it be sold? Should there be an environmental or societal bid? "Sure, exactly," he says. "It is the responsibility of governments to put themselves in the position of the people they're representing. That's what the job is. That's a tautology. Put themselves in the position of the people they represent and ask the question: Well, this tree that's been here for those hundreds of years, just how much money would the people of NSW want me to charge for somebody taking this tree?"

Is that happening today? Is somebody making that sort of bid? "Look it's better but it's ... that's all I'd be prepared to say in respect of royalties ... It's better." As a sign of change Henry nominates the petroleum resource rent tax, which has behind it, he says, "precisely the thinking that I've been talking about."

But how would that help preserve the dodo when the collectors looked at their costs of getting to the islands, collecting the dodos and making a bit of a profit and were unaware that they were harvesting the last bird? He agrees there are no environmentalists putting in the bid to preserve the bird.

So is this a problem for these sort of environmental assets? "Absolutely it is. There is a role for governments in that area. Governments – we're going back a long way now – but Australian governments are culpable for the extinction of the thylacine and I think it's something like 110, or 120 species of Australian flora and fauna that have been made extinct since the time of white settlement. Australian governments have a responsibility for that. They're culpable for that ... They're responsible, not only to look after the interests of the present generation of voters but future generations as well. Who else can put themselves in that position? I mean it's too much to expect people like my ancestors who harvested red cedar on the north coast of NSW, it's a bit much to expect them, on their own, not to take out so many trees on the basis of concern for future generations having access to red cedar. But it is not a bit much, surely, to expect a government to look after the interests of future generations."

So is he an environmentalist or the head of Treasury? "I think most heads of Treasury, most of my 14 predecessors, would have been environmentalists in this sense." Henry says one economist who has influenced his thinking more than any other is Nobel Prize winning, Amartya Sen. Sen, he says, proposes that people should have the capabilities to choose lives that they have reason to value. "Now, without a decent education, without decent health, you can't say that people have the capability to choose a life that they have reason to value. Those are fundamental ... we could have a debate about to what level, obviously; and what sort of education, obviously. But they're second order issues for this discussion."

He refers favourably to Sen's article, *Why We Should Save the Spotted Owl,* and says that in it he talks about the concept of sustainable development. "Nobel prize winning economists back in the sixties and seventies were talking about sustainable development in terms of every future generation having a standard of living at least as high as the present generation. Sen says that's not enough."

"What do you mean by standard of living? If you're going to measure standard of living in terms of only material wealth and incomes, then Sen would demur. He would say that there is an argument for protecting the spotted owl that has nothing to do with preservation of the standard of living. And it is that the present generation has the capability to enjoy the existence of the spotted owl ... Future generations should also have that capability – well Sen uses the word freedom – to enjoy the existence, to appreciate the existence, of the spotted owl. And so I would say the same thing with respect to the thylacine. I'd say it with respect to the northern hairy nosed wombat that is now on death row."

Henry agrees that this relates to the level to which we consume forests and the resources of the seas and the environments in which spotted owls live. "All I'm saying is that government has a role in this. It's an appropriate role of government. And that governments should not practice benign neglect, or even worse, actually participate in destruction."

Henry says he was initially interested in economics because of the intellectual challenge. After completing an honours degree at the University of NSW he was invited by his supervisor, the late Professor Richard Manning, to do a PhD at Canterbury University in New Zealand where Manning had taken a chair. Henry's two children were born there while he lectured and continued his studies. "Those were tough years," he says. "I was a lecturer in economics in New Zealand in the last years of the Muldoon Government. And the Muldoon Government was a disgrace. In almost any terms, but certainly in economic policy terms, it was a disgrace."

Although Henry's thesis was highly theoretical and mathematical he says he found himself getting involved in and eventually becoming motivated by real world policy issues. Looking back across the Tasman he saw what was happening, particularly when the Hawke Government was elected in 1983, and he applied for a job with the Australian Treasury working on tax. With tax reform a major issue on the political agenda for the next twenty years, he was destined to occupy positions which could not go unnoticed.

When the Coalition Government was elected in 1996, Henry would have been an unlikely prospect as a future head of Treasury. A highly qualified Division Head and professional public servant he might well have been, but his close working relationship with Labor guaranteed long odds on the Coalition offering him the top job five years later. "Initially, I'd have to say, my relationship with the Government was a bit tense," he says. This is hardly surprising. Henry joined Tax Policy Division in 1984 at the executive level and moved across to Labor Treasurer Paul Keating's office in 1986. Over the years when the Coalition was in Opposition he worked on tax models, including the model that played a key role in destroying former Opposition Leader, John Hewson's *Fightback!* economic package. "Over time they obviously grew comfortable with me," he says.

Henry experienced the full roller coaster of major tax change events that occurred from the mid-1980s to today. The year he joined Treasury he was right in the middle of the small team of officers putting together the Government's white paper on tax reform that went to the tax summit in 1985. "We were putting that together confronting absolutely impossible deadlines," he says. "We were working crazy hours through the night … [with] kids sleeping under desks." Henry's children were four and five at the time. "I don't think there was any case where I brought my kids in and they slept right through. But there were times when they were there sleeping until late in the night."

Henry says he did not see a lot of his kids growing up and this was a huge loss'. He observes that he was not unlike his father but says it has had an interesting effect on his son who is now 24 and, has two university degrees. "He's not quite sure what he wants to do with his life and the reason is that he saw first hand the sort of life I had." He notes that there were a number of periods when he was working 100 hours a week and says the impact on his family was "Pretty bad" but his wife was understanding – "more than I could reasonably have expected." Henry's Division Head in the mid-1980s was David Morgan, now head of Westpac. Henry would typically work on a tax draft and slip it under Morgan's front door by 3 am. Morgan would get up and read it and have dealt with it by 8 am.

Despite all the work, Keating's preferred Option C tax package did not win the support of the Tax Summit. Henry says this was "almost soul destroying … along with the others in the team, I had invested everything … I knew as soon as Bob White, who was chairman of the Business Council of Australia, got to his feet and said, 'Business Council doesn't like option A. Business Council doesn't like Option B. And Business Council doesn't like option C'."

"We were listening to this over the in-house service in the old Parliament House and I turned to the others and said, 'Well that's that'." That was on the morning of the Summit. After lunch the Prime Minister, Bob Hawke, announced that the Government would not proceed with Option C. Henry says the support of the business community had pretty much been taken for granted and they had thought the problem was going to be getting the support of the ACTU. "Now of course the Business Council didn't support it at the time … because Option C contained Option A with the income tax base-broadening measures of fringe benefits tax, capital gains tax and so on … Well, of course, the business community didn't want any of that, did they? But what an extraordinary blunder from the Business Council because Keating needed nobody's support to legislate fringe benefits tax and capital gains tax [and] of course that's what he did … on the last night of the Summit [Keating] got us together in his office in old

Parliament House and he said, 'Look, we're going to push on. We've lost the consumption tax. But we're going to push on. We are going to get the fringe benefits tax and the capital gains tax and so on. And nobody can stop us'. And so we did."

Hawke had always said unless there was community support for Option C he would not proceed with it. "That's right; that's fair enough I suppose," Henry says. "But you don't just get the support by publishing something and waiting for people to tell you how good it is. And Hawke knew that ... he knew that getting support for the position involved an element of hard work ... he didn't bear any scars from it at all. None at all. Keating bore all the scars."

Henry stayed in the team designing the fringe benefits tax and the capital gains tax that appeared in the September 1985 tax reform package. He spent the next year helping with implementation of the package before moving to Keating's office where he stayed for nearly five years until Keating lost his first challenge for leadership of the Government in June 1991. "Those were extraordinary years", he says.

Keating had made his statement that Australia was in danger of becoming a Banana Republic shortly before Henry joined his office and economic policy dominated the political agenda during his time in the office. Despite the pressure of work in the office Henry says "I'd be very surprised if you would find anybody who had ever worked for Keating in his office who had a bad thing to say about him." Asked why he had this level of support, he says, "He valued people and you knew that you were valued. He was inclusive. He discussed all sorts of issues with people in the office ... at least in the office he never pushed his view down anybody else's throat. I often saw the opposite, that is, attempts by people in the office ... to push views down his throat. And he'd sit and he'd listen and he'd take it. And sometimes he'd agree and sometimes he'd say, 'well ...' There was always a healthy debate in the office."

After Keating lost his first challenge in June 1991, he retired to the backbench before mounting a second challenge in December of that year, which he won. John Kerin had replaced Keating as Treasurer, but he in turn had been replaced by Ralph Willis in December. When Keating won the prime ministership, he appointed John Dawkins as Treasurer and they mounted an attack on Opposition Leader John Hewson's Fightback! tax reform election package.

While Keating was sitting on the backbench, Kerin instructed his department to build a capacity to quantify the price, revenue and distributional implications of any indirect tax change. Henry, with his academic tax-modelling background and previous Treasury tax experience, was appointed to lead the Treasury team to develop this modelling capacity. He was given half a dozen people and told to build the modelling capacity in four months. In the end it took five.

"It was like 1985 all over again. But in other ways it couldn't have been more different … The way in which it was the same was that the deadline was impossible. And so we were working absurd hours … again it was 100 hours a week stuff. But it was completely unlike 1985 in the sense that we were not helping the Government to develop a positive package. Kerin had never said to the department, 'I'm going to use this to monster Hewson's tax package when he gets it out.' Although he'd never said that, we knew, obviously, what it was going to be used to do. We knew that Hewson's package was going to include a broad based consumption tax, the thing which in 1985 we were helping the Government to design. So you could say that our hearts were not in the job. But we nevertheless had an instruction from the Government. 'You do it'."

Did anyone think of saying, this is improper to do? "Look, in the department there was quite a discussion about that issue. And I'm sure there are bits of paper that deal with that question of whether it's proper or improper to do, but the view that was taken in the department, from the Secretary down, was there was no basis on which we could refuse to do this. And that's true. If I were to get an instruction from the Federal Treasurer – and the instruction from Kerin was in writing – today, 'I want you to do X', unless it's illegal, I turn to section 57 of the Public Service Act and that says it is the responsibility of the Secretary, under the minister, to manage the department."

"That's very clear. Unless it's illegal you do it. And that's part of being a professional public servant … if you think that it shouldn't be done for some broader policy reason, philosophical reason, political reason, whatever, you simply have to put that aside. And here was a case where not only did we not want to see this done, because we knew for what purpose it was going to be used and we didn't think that was a good policy purpose. We had invested a large part of our souls in the particular policy objective in 1985. Nevertheless we were being told, 'You've got to do this'. And as professional public servants we did it."

When Fightback! came out, the model the team had developed enabled the identification of a major failing in the package. Income tax bracket creep had been used to fund the package but bracket creep had not been used in the analysis of the after tax income various taxpayers would receive. Treasury was accused by the Coalition of having acted improperly. "We did not act improperly," Henry says. "We rejected that charge at the time. I would always reject it. There was nothing improper in what we did. But it is the case that our work was used by the Government to attack publicly an Opposition policy. That's just the fact of it. And the great irony, of course, in this for me personally is that then 1997 comes along and the Prime Minister, Prime Minister Howard, wants me as chairman of the Government's Taxation Taskforce to develop the

GST that we now have. So I've seen all sides. It's been, I have to say, a huge emotional rollercoaster."

Henry says he's never discussed why he was appointed by the Prime Minister to that role but "I'm sure the way the Prime Minister would have looked at it is that if there's anybody in Australia who can see a chink in the thing, it's going to be this bloke. That's probably the way that his mind worked. Anyway, had I been in his shoes that's what I would have thought."

So Henry got another team together and brushed the cobwebs off his Prismod model they had built in 1991. Prismod had taken 12 hours to run the first time it operated and was a nightmare. "Literally a nightmare," says Henry, "because I would set the alarm at home for 2 o'clock or 3 o'clock in the morning, come into the office and check whether it had crashed or not. If it had crashed I'd set it going again so that by 8 o'clock we could check it again. But by 1998 it could be run in one and a half minutes."

Despite the Government's commitment to the GST, not everything ran smoothly. The Government did not have control of the Senate and initially sought the support of Tasmanian independent, Senator Brian Harradine. "I was travelling with Costello when Harradine said that he couldn't support it," Henry says.

"I think we were in Singapore on our way, I can't remember to where … and he got the call that Harradine had finally stood up and said that, in all conscience, he couldn't support a GST. I thought, 'I've been through this before. I've seen this before'. It's difficult for me to put myself in Costello's shoes, and I try not to … but I'm sure had I been in his shoes I would have said, 'I'm just not going to go on with this. Forget it. It's gone'." But, to his credit, Henry says, Costello kept going. The end result was a deal that saw the GST introduced with food excluded. "Is a GST without food as good as a GST with food? In my view, No, if only for the compliance issues involved. But is a GST without food better than no GST at all? Yes. And, as I said, to Costello's great credit he continued to push on with it and we got it."

Henry says that usually governments which introduce such taxes are defeated in the next election but the Coalition government was not defeated. He says this in part may have been because it was well implemented. Both the IMF and the OECD have said that the implementation of the Australian GST was a model for other countries. "In terms of its impact on the economy it was an absolute textbook case," he says. "We drew pictures for the Government showing what we thought the time path for the CPI [consumer price index] effect was going to be. And when we got the actual figures and you laid them over the top you'd scarcely see daylight between the two lines."

Henry maintains that the economic policy settings are absolutely fundamental to the strong performance of the economy. "Running disciplined medium term fiscal policy doesn't happen by accident", he says. "And it certainly doesn't happen without Treasury … it certainly doesn't happen either without the right micro-policy settings, without an appropriate tax system, without the right regulatory structures in the financial system, which is Treasury responsibility, and corporate governance and competition policy which are Treasury responsibilities. In most of those areas we have the responsibility ourselves to develop policy and I would say that in most of those areas – financial regulation, corporate governance, competition policy – certainly in those areas the policy settings in Australia are widely regarded around the world as world's best practice. And that's got a lot to do with Treasury."

He also points out that one of his *ex officio* roles is to sit on the Reserve Bank Board which sets interest rates. This workload places strains on the agency of 800 people. Henry says the way that they are funded, where an efficiency dividend requires a cut in administrative costs each year, requires the department to reduce staff numbers by about 30 people a year. This requires a rate of productivity growth that is about double that in the private sector, he says. He recognises that the public sector does not have the market discipline that exists for businesses. The Government exerts the discipline. It decides what price it is going to pay for services.

As head of Treasury Henry is in one of the key service positions to present a policy alternative, so does he have anything else in mind? "Not yet. But I'm thinking about it," he says. Another serious issue he nominates for the department is freedom of information requests about the development of government policy. "The way this is going, there are only two possible consequences I can see for this department," he says. "I'm satisfied, having reviewed a number of them, that by and large they have been motivated by a desire to either embarrass the Government and Treasurer, or the department. Now it is not my role to help people embarrass the Government. So how am I going to respond? There are two likely responses. The first is that you will see Conclusive Certificates, stating conclusively that it is not in the public interest for the information to be released, issued on every one of them. That's very likely."

The second response, which he says is already happening, is that documents will not be produced. Communication on sensitive policy issues will be verbal. "Communication with the Treasurer is obviously vital. But, because of FOI, records are not always kept." Yet Henry says he thinks it is "very important that records are kept of oral communication with ministers and ministers' offices and that there is an accurate recording of not just the decision, but the considerations underlying the decision. It's very important."

FOI requests cannot be made for Cabinet documents but Henry says he cannot just stamp Cabinet-In-Confidence on a document to keep it private. "It has to be a document of the Cabinet which seems to mean that at least it has been noted in the Cabinet decision. Well, I can't remember a Treasury briefing to a Treasurer for a cabinet meeting that's ever been noted in a Cabinet decision. So somebody needs to think through the implications of the increasingly aggressive use of FOI for record keeping in departments like this one. And I can tell you it is having an adverse impact on record keeping. There are documents that are simply not being prepared. It's an issue."

This article was first published in the Canberra Times on 23 January 2006

The Devil's Advocate – Ian Watt, Department of Finance and Administration

The Budget, according to the head of the Department of Finance and Administration, Dr Ian Watt, is the biggest single thing that Government does year in, year out. So it is not the sort of place you want to make a mistake when you are a rising young section head in the Treasury department. And if you make a mistake, the worst time to find it must be around 4 pm on Budget day when the media lock-up is underway and it is only a matter of hours before the Treasurer, Paul Keating, rises to deliver his statement on the new direction for the economy.

But that is precisely the situation Dr Watt found himself in as an executive officer responsible for the Budget speech in 1986. "I think that was close to my worst day in the public service", he says. "I mean Treasury treated ... these things as something close to Holy Writ – the Budget speech is very, very important. It had to be right. Now we couldn't correct that error. It was too late. The thing had been printed. It was in the lock-up." No corrigendum was issued. Treasurer Keating simply didn't deliver the offending sentence when speaking in the House later that night.

"What did that teach me?" Watt asks. "What the relevant person in the then Department of Finance who was clearing the speech had been trying to tell us was that there was a mistake. They hadn't actually said so in so many words. They had been re-writing the sentence. We in Treasury thought their change was only stylistic. And, therefore, we'd been re-writing it back again. What that taught me was to think carefully about what people tell me."

Watt was appointed Secretary of the Department of Finance and Administration in January 2002, after nearly a year as Secretary of the Department of Communications, Information, Technology and the Arts. Born in Preston, in Victoria, and an only child whose mother died when he was young, Watt came to Canberra in 1973 after a year as a Treasury cadet when he completed a Bachelor of Commerce degree with honours. But Watt's public service career was interrupted when his father became ill and he decided to go back to Melbourne to look after him. In Melbourne he pursued his studies, completing his masters and his doctorate at La Trobe University where he taught for ten years. In 1977 his father died but it was not until 1985 that Watt returned to the public service in Canberra.

Watt says outside Canberra people tend to think that the Budget is all Treasury's work. But other public servants know that one of Finance's key roles is its work on the Budget. The separation is not always clear, but broadly speaking Treasury does the macro-economic side and revenue, and Finance does expenses, non-tax revenue and the accounting. Watt says that for part of the year Finance seems to work as much with the Treasurer as with the Minister for Finance.

Apart from the Budget, Finance is also responsible for the Government's financial framework, maintenance of the Government's financial accounts, management of a small property portfolio, advice on government business enterprises, an assets sales taskforce and ministerial and parliamentary services to Members, Senators and their staff. Most recently the department has also become home to the Australian Government Information Management Office, which is responsible for providing whole of government advice on information technology issues.

To other departments, Finance is the bogeyman agency, the department that critiques, and often opposes, their spending proposals. "You would always expect departments ... to be enthusiastic about spending on their programs", Watt says. "You would also always expect that not everyone would share all of their enthusiasm."

He rejects any suggestion that Finance automatically adopts a "No, or less" position on these proposals. "I'd say to people, Finance should never be afraid to support a good investment ... but it's got to be a good investment. And a good investment doesn't mean one that the department concerned supports, or thinks is important. Nor does a good investment necessarily mean – even if you accept that in terms of the department's own priorities it's the right thing – it doesn't necessarily mean in terms of the whole of government priorities, it's the right thing."

He says Finance not surprisingly often comes out with a somewhat smaller sense of what's highly desirable expenditure. "But when you look at it, we don't say no or less to every proposal." Do you ever say more? "Yes, on occasions, we have. I don't think there are many but I can remember four or five in the last couple of years in which we've been prepared to do that. Now they'd be the exception, not the rule. Equally there are a lot of proposals that we actually support."

Watt says the discussions between departments are conducted in a thoroughly professional fashion. "We have different points of view on some issues", he says. "That's fine. That's expected. We conduct ourselves professionally on all occasions and I believe other departments do the same."

He says his staff sometimes come to him over a difference of opinion where another department Secretary might wish to talk to him. " I would always take the call if it was made (often it's not), listen to the issue that was raised with me, think about it, talk to my officers and go back. You won't be surprised that normally I would support my officers' positions but I'm no rubber stamp. I would always think about what any of my senior colleagues from other departments say to me. I have never felt that any of my colleagues would pressure me unreasonably or unfairly or at all, to change my department's views because it suited them. I think they respect our views on saying 'No' sometimes, just as we respect their views of putting forward good ideas to government. It's just that we can't afford all of the good ideas."

The other big ticket item currently consuming Finance time is its responsibility for T3, the Telstra share sale. T3 is the largest, or the second largest single Australian share offer, and Finance is responsible for providing advice on the sale. To do this it will engage global co-ordinators who will be three or four major investment banks who will run the sale. All contracts will be with the department or under its authority. The global co-ordinators, who are best placed to know the market, will provide advice on the share price and all other aspects of the sale, and the department will then advise the minister responsible for the sale, Senator Nick Minchin.

Watt says the thing he is most proud of is being a leader in the Australian Public Service but he adds that, "being a Secretary doesn't make you a leader." Leadership to Watt is having a vision about where the organisation should go. "I emphasise to my people all the way down the chain, we're all leaders, in our own field," he says.

Asked about the constraints imposed by government he says that one has to operate by definition within the broad framework that government sets for the department and the public service. "It's not much good me having a vision of Finance being something that does all these wonderful things if the Government is not interested. But virtually every leader operates within a constraint. Within that framework I have a wide scope, flexibility to set a vision and an agenda for my organisation."

If, for example the Government wanted Finance to be tough on budgetary issues, what would that mean? "Does that mean I create an organisation which is expert at mugging people on the way to the cabinet room? I don't believe I do that. Do I create an organisation which has the intellectual horsepower to argue with their counterparts about what is necessary spending, what's not, what's high priority, what's not. That's what I try to create."

This article was first published in the Canberra Times on 21 November 2005

Starting from Scratch – Patricia Scott, Department of Human Services

Patricia Scott got the good news in mid-October 2004. "You've been promoted to department head." And the bad news a second later. She would be heading a department that didn't exist! Scott was one of four women whose promotion was announced on Friday 22 October. The other three moved into well-established positions with the full support of staff and established practices.

In her new role Scott was called first by her minister. "Then I went and checked with Peter (Shergold, the head of the Department of the Prime Minister and Cabinet) on the time I was supposed to start. To be frank he hadn't said when. And it was Friday that it was publicly announced. We started formally – we got the instrument – on the 26th, so I think there was the weekend and the Monday and that was the total preparation we had."

On Tuesday Scott found herself with her executive assistant, Jacqueline O'Brien, and her executive officer, Alison McCann, in a room with three desks and chairs in the Minter Ellison building in Barton. "It was amazing, very challenging, very daunting," she says. "We checked that the telephones worked and started inviting people in … and then we'd say 'look can you stay, can you stay today?' And then we'd say 'can you stay this week?'"

For anyone who has worked in the public service and knows all the governance requirements and protocols, it is hard to over-state the difficulties she faced. The growing Human Services department would need more space and would have to move. But even the basics had their difficulties. To get a post office box, which would provide at least one fixed point, you need to be able to identify who you are. And for this you need an Australian Business Number.

"Well, we didn't have a bank account. We didn't have an ABN, we didn't have a fixed address. We didn't have any bills sent to us," Scott said. But in government there is no time out. From day one finances must be arranged, accountability requirements apply, the new minister must be serviced, staff must be paid, an IT system must be provided and security arrangements must work.

The Estimates Committee hearings were due to start in five weeks. "We didn't have the people to say 'Fred, what did we do last time?'" Scott says. "There was no last time." Support from other departments was essential. Scott said she needed to travel to Sydney to meet the minister but didn't have any means to fund the flight so "someone paid our airfare." Departments were more than happy to lend staff for a week, but not so keen if the period was going to extend to three, or six, months.

They needed a lawyer and by the end of the week had one on secondment. Attorney-Generals' visited and were told of the governance issues. "Their eyes got larger and larger and larger and they said, 'well we'll send someone over this afternoon'."

With security, Scott says she got lucky. "I ended up having someone I knew who had a very good strong record on security so by about the end of week one, or week two, I had a security officer." They had to deal with Cabinet documents but some staff were not familiar with the requirements. They acquired a fire engine red lockable cabinet and the security officer began the process of getting clearances for other staff.

They had to write all manuals from scratch. "I handed someone a Cabinet submission and I said, 'Can you please keep the co-ord comment short?' and he said 'Yep'. And he walked about three steps and he said 'What's a co-ord comment?'"

Initially the Department of the Prime Minister and Cabinet looked after the few office staff. At the time of her promotion Scott was a Deputy Secretary in PM&C and the department kept her, and her immediate staff, on the payroll. "We've paid them back now, obviously", she says. "We took people on an unfunded secondment basis and now have met those bills."

Borrowed staff created spread sheets to record initial transactions. A *jerry-built* computer system provided basic services. A major initial task was to get funding for the new department. Human Services was set up to oversee six service delivery agencies, including the giant Centrelink, Medicare Australia and the Child Support Agency. These agencies are contracted by policy departments such as the Department of Health and Ageing, or the Department of Family and Community Services, to provide services for their clients.

No additional Budget funding was provided for the new Human Services department. Funding was to come from the policy departments. This required negotiation with them on how much each would contribute. Scott says one of the things she had to do was explain very carefully her department's purpose. In doing this she was greatly assisted by the statements made by Mr Howard and Dr Shergold on the day of her appointment. The result of these negotiations was an $8 million department which has now increased to around $12 million due to extra responsibilities it has acquired.

In his initial statement Mr Howard said Human Services would improve the delivery of services and ensure that the Government got best value for money. Scott says although hers is not a policy department, it has a role in seeing that service delivery issues are considered in the development of policy. But if this is so, why not simply have representatives of the delivery agencies included in the policy development committees? "We're not trying to be a third wheel, or get in the way of good communications between policy departments and service delivery," Scott says. "In fact we're trying to facilitate those discussions."

She says there will always be a need to consider the balance of interests between the policy departments and the delivery agencies and "I think that's where we come into it. Sometimes we're going to be batting with the agencies, and sometimes we're going to be batting with the policy departments." But the Human Services role which the six agencies operating under its umbrella might fear is the role of overseer or accountability master. Scott says it is undoubtedly the case that one of Human Services' functions is to increase accountability. "That's one of the things the Prime Minister said the department was about," she says.

This is one of the reason why the agencies under Human Services have been the first to implement the Uhrig reforms. These reforms, recommended by former Westpac chairman John Uhrig, called for clear lines of responsibility in agencies and proposed that a number of boards that ran agencies should be abolished. The boards running the Health Insurance Commission, now renamed Medicare Australia, and Centrelink have now gone. "We are about improved accountability," Scott says. "We are about wanting to know more about how things are done and why they're done that way and could they become better? What are the queue times? And what's the wait time? And how many calls don't get answered? I'm not going to apologise for that. These are very large organisations delivering lots and lots of services and we haven't hit Nirvana. Every now and again we've got to say to an agency, 'you've got to lift your game'. And every now and again we've got to say to the policy departments, 'Be reasonable. You can't expect a service if you're not prepared to fund that service'."

Scott acknowledges that she is dealing with human organisations which sometimes excel and sometimes don't deliver as expected. She says her department is hopefully a good rational body that can run on to the field and bring the players together in a way that meets the common goals, "but they won't always view things exactly the same way."

She says the structure they have is a novel arrangement. "I feel like we're the McKinseys of service delivery. We're not trying to do all the service delivery ourselves. We want to be small. We want to be fleet of foot and we want to get on top of an issue and then leave it to other people to get on with. We want to broker solutions and see points of co-ordination." She suggests, for example, that some agencies have excellent records in low turnover or low Comcare insurance premiums, low absenteeism and others have very high Comcare premiums, high absenteeism.

The diverse experience and expertise can be shared to benefit all. Since its establishment the department has been given some additional responsibility –

the preparation of Comprehensive Work Capacity Assessments. To back up the Government's Welfare to Work program, Human Services has been asked to design a process to assess the capacity to work of people on disability support pension or NewStart allowance. The process will use people who can assess disabilities, such as psychologists and occupational therapists.

The department is looking at ways to reduce queues and cut the number of letters agencies send out. Centrelink, for example sends out 90 million letters a year. Alternatives, such as the use of SMS, or online systems, to inform people of an appointment or undertake transactions, are being considered. "We're not about one monolithic way of dealing with things," Scott says. "You know if a new baby's born, the parent has to give the basic information to Medicare Australia. Isn't it sensible that Medicare Australia, with their permission, passes that on to Centrelink?"

"This is a novel, small department and its got to be dynamic", she says. "I don't want to ossify into a large organisation trying to cover absolutely everything because that will detract from the service delivery ... and make us less relevant."

Scott probably took the prize for extreme public service working hours in the lead up to Christmas 2004. "I got caught out one morning because I came in early and got stuck in the lift," she says. "I had to call the service man at 5 am. It was very rugged – pretty full on." From her appointment in October until Christmas she frequently worked until 11 pm. But she did have a week of planned leave. "I'm a big believer in holidays."

Scott says she "likes a challenge" and believes she was chosen for the job because she had been in PM&C working in social policy and was familiar with some of the service delivery issues that the Government had been grappling with. Scott is an economist by training and has worked on policy development and program delivery. She jokes that she started off the job 12 months ago as a brunette (not quite true) and has ended up white haired.

She says her management style is enthusiastic and she thinks she motivates people. "I think I'm clear in what I expect," she says. "I like working closely with other people. I like working with teams. I'm not aloof." She points out that she got rid of the wall that a previous department had erected between the executive area she inhabits and the open staff area. "I thought it was ridiculous," she says.

In a moment of reflection she says, "Maybe I would have been luckier if I'd got a department which had a 50 year track record. On the other hand, if we've done it well then we can take credit, and it we've stuffed it up – and occasionally we have – well it's our responsibility." She is hands on but says she cannot be a micro-manager when she heads a department that looks after agencies employing 37,000 people. "You can't micro manage six CEOs simultaneously.

And you can't micro manage a really busy, even little, department. The day to day management of Centrelink is entirely the responsibility of Jeff Whalan The responsibility for Child Support is entirely Matt Miller. But in terms of co-ordination, in terms of are they keeping on the task that the Government wants them to, that's a role I have to play."

She says if she had her time again she would have spent a bit more time explaining, especially to people who were feeling anxious about what the changes the creation of Human Services meant. Asked if she is referring to the heads of the six agencies, she says, "Sometimes the heads of the agencies, sometimes I'm talking about the policy departments themselves, 'cause not everyone's reading Shergold's speech and not everyone's got the time or the inclination to look at the PM's website. So a lot of time was spent initially on what's the difference between policy and service delivery. But, when it's all said and done, it's like trying to divide the ingredients in a chocolate cake. It's the two things coming together that make the cake."

This article was first published in the Canberra Times on 28 November 2005

The Reluctant Chief – Ric Smith, Department of Defence

The Defence department's annual report does not specify who is paid what, but in an appendix it sets out, in $10,000 pay brackets, the total remuneration for all those getting $100,000 or more. The top paid executive receives between $590,000 and $599,999. Another is in the pay bracket $560,000 to $569,999 and the third highest is in the bracket $470,000 to $479,999. These figures are not straight salary, but include the value of other benefits such as the provision of housing to defence personnel.

This led Ric Smith to quip that the published figure included the "accrued value of the view from my toilet." Smith is paid his salary for running an organisation where life and death decisions may have to be made, where 90,000 people are employed and $54 billion of assets are managed and where 20 million shareholders are serviced by endless scrutiny of his agency's actions. When asked why he takes on such a demanding job, he says it is worthwhile. He does not complain about his pay and even says he is "well paid". But how well?

The *Australian Financial Review* published a list of the pay packages of private sector CEOs last month. None would have anywhere near the relentless workload and pressures that Smith encounters in his job and there are questions about whether any of their salaries are justified. But taking the figures at face value they show the average pay for heads of the top 300 listed companies at a staggering $1.9 million. In cash terms these chief executives took home an average $1.5 million in salaries, benefits and bonuses. This excludes the accounting value attached to options and other equity incentives.

US-based News Ltd chief Rupert Murdoch pocketed $23.6 million. Macquarie Bank chief Allan Morris received a salary of $659,323 and a 'short-term incentive' of $17,436,757. Poor Toll chief, Paul Little, only thirtieth, taking home $4.4 million.

The head of the Defence Materials Organisation, Dr Steve Gumley, who was recruited from the private sector after rising through Australian companies to become Vice President Information Services with the Boeing Company, has no doubt that Smith is not properly remunerated for the responsibility he carries.

"No! not even close," he says. "I look at the working hours and the pressures of the senior executives in Defence and I compare it with the senior executives in defence companies and the reward/risk work-profile are very, very different. You could add a zero to the secretary's salary and probably be fairly accurate to what the private sector would pay for a similar role," he says. "I can compare and contrast and I would view the workload and responsibility of the Secretary of the Department of Defence as at least the equal of the chief executive of any of the top companies in Australia. It's hours, it's availability, it's responsibility for people of our country, it's the life and death issues of deployment ..."

On the Defence Materials Organisation side of the department the figures make the private sector's activities in Australia pale into insignificance. Gumley says they spend about $3.7 to $3.8 billion a year on the major projects. But because many projects last five, ten or fifteen years the added commitments are up around $30 billion at any one time. A private company such as Telstra might from time to time have a bigger project in a particular year but, as Gumley points out, Defence does it year after year after year.

"We've got an acquisition program which is made up of 220 major projects. There's 100 minor projects. And we also have to maintain approximately 100 fleets. We use the word fleet to mean a fleet of F18 jet fighters, or a fleet of FFG destroyers. We run about 100 different fleets and we're spending about $3.3 or $3.4 billion a year maintaining those fleets. I've been chief executive of private sector companies a few times. The work here is significantly longer and harder than anything I've experienced in the private sectorm" Gumley says, and then quickly adds, "I'm not complaining."

Smith observes that over the 37 years he has been in the Commonwealth Public Service he has seen work "sucked upwards". "The more attentive ministers are to the detail of the portfolio, the more the Secretary will be drawn in," he said. "[P]eople talk about the politicisation in the public service. I don't think that's the issue. I think the issue, to be frank, is that ministers themselves are much more involved in their portfolios than they were ... when I joined the public service." He says the level of scrutiny is "enormous". "There is no question that work is drawn upwards by this process," he says. "You could say that it's poor delegation, or poor time management. Or you could say it's the more effective working of the parliamentary system."

The range of issues he has to master and the significance of them is hard to comprehend. He notes, for example, that Defence is the biggest producer of greenhouse gases in the Commonwealth. Someone will have a plan to diminish this and want to talk to him about it. "It's tempting to say, 'I don't do that'. But I'm kind of interested and you want to know about it."

Or it could be a health and safety issue. Or an issue to do with the military justice system. Or an issue to do with the accounts which still suffer from the Auditor General's qualification. Gumley points out that he's got four domain managers in DMO each managing a billion dollar business. "I regard them as the equivalent of chief executives of major supply companies," he says. "The Band 1 and Band 2 SES officers here work long hours with a lot of responsibility and any bashing of public servants is totally unwarranted."

Smith has been appointed to the top job in Defence for another two years but there is no guarantee he will see out the term. Responding to the extension of his three year contract he said he was honoured to be reappointed but with the Prime Minister, Mr Howard's support, he had requested the option of retirement within this period. Smith, who turns 62 in March 2005, has been in the public service for 37 years. "This time next year I'll be approaching 63 and I now have a grandchild and I just don't want to work forever so I'll keep it under review," he said.

Smith acknowledges that his job imposes a strain on his work/life balance but takes the view that his is a worthwhile job that deserves a lot of time and attention. "There are 90,000 people to whom it matters and there are lives involved in it, and massive amounts of money," he says. "It just deserves and needs a lot of attention. Secondly, I'm well paid. And thirdly my family is grown up. So long as my wife and I understand this, then we can cope. I wouldn't want to be doing this job and having young kids I'd have to take to sport, or music or whatever."

As a diplomat in the Department of Foreign Affairs and Trade in 1996 Smith considered his retirement options and thought he would do a couple of assignments as an ambassador – Government willing – and then retire at maybe 60 or 61. Everything was going to plan. He was appointed ambassador to China from 1996 to 2000 and then ambassador to Indonesia for 2001-02. "Then I was asked if I would do this job and I had to re-think what the remaining 20 years of my life might look like."

Have you made the right decision? "In many ways yes," he says. "But the demands have been great ... there might have been moments, I'll confess, when I've regretted it ... there have been some pretty hectic times in the Senate Estimates as you know. There were some pretty demanding times in regard to our financial statements. And in this organisation, there's always something going on somewhere that will surprise you."

Smith says Defence is the last of the great old departments that did almost everything itself. At the same time it is one of Australia's largest corporations. There are 90,000 people including reservists, plus 10,000 contractors doing things that staff and service personnel used to do like mowing lawns around the bases. Defence occupies 450 sites around Australia and is one of Australia's biggest land owners. It concludes about 5000 contracts of $100,000 or more a year. It holds $54 billion worth of assets and has $7 billion worth of liabilities. Smith says these are enormous figures in Australian terms, "so it's not like being the secretary of most departments".

Under the *Financial Management Act* Smith is the chief executive officer of Defence. "Sort of makes me chief clerk," he says, but then adds that he is also the principal civilian adviser to the Minister for Defence. Smith is responsible for the administration of the department, the Defence Science and Technology Organisation and the three intelligence agencies. He is jointly responsible, with the Chief of the Defence Force, Air Chief Marshal Angus Houston, for the administration of the Australian Defence Force.

Every day he talks to Houston who occupies an adjoining office. "There are chunks of work that are clearly his – military operations – and there are chunks of work that are clearly mine – financial management issues," he says. "And then there's a whole breadth of work in the middle that belongs to both of us. But we support each other in the exclusive areas, so in military operations, I attend all the Strategic Command Group meetings. And in the financial administration both Peter Cosgrove [the former Chief of the Defence Force] and Angus Houston have been tremendously supportive."

Smith was awarded the Public Service Medal for outstanding service as Australian Ambassador leading Australia's response in Indonesia following the Bali bombing on 12 October 2002. On the Saturday night of the bombing he was in Djakarta attending his farewell party. Within minutes of hearing of the blasts any thought of departure was put on hold. For three weeks he oversaw operations in Bali which at one stage involved a couple of hundred Australian officials.

Not all his diplomatic work has been as worthy or up-lifting. He admits that he missed a minister at the airport once – always a risky business for a diplomat. He had driven himself to the airport to save on calling a driver out at midnight and then had a problem parking. The lesson he says he learnt from this was "don't cut the little corners." As for other mistakes, he says that sometimes he has delegated work when he should have done it himself. "You're at the end of the day, and you're just too tired, and you've asked someone to do it and it goes wrong."

He says he has only ever had one really nasty manager. "He was just an unpleasant man who saw himself testing people all the time," he says. "He'd tell you later, 'well I put that on you just to see how you'd cope'. I just don't like that kind of game playing. It might have been more common years ago but I don't think it happens much now."

To do his job Smith starts at about 7 am and "I finish when I finish." He nominates three major challenges for the department at the moment. Firstly, sustaining operations and giving the most effective and efficient services support possible to Australia's deployed forces and ensuring that they are well prepared. The second is ensuring that Defence is playing the right role in national security management. "The time was when you thought security, you thought Defence Force," he says. "Not now. Many other agencies are involved as well as Defence." There is a new set of policies that require the correct positioning of the intelligence agencies, science and technology and the Defence Force. "I'm happy with where we are, the Chief is, the minister is, but it's a constantly changing environment."

The third great challenge is improving the efficiency of the organisation. "Defence organisations – this one in particular – have historically been marvellously effective, but not so efficient." Getting efficient is difficult for a number of reasons. One is that Defence has always been judged by, and valued for, its effectiveness, rather than efficiency. It did not matter if the job cost more as long as it was done. "We're a very unusual organisation in today's world," he says. "We're a just-in-case organisation in a just-in-time world." Modern management did not readily cater for that.

"Because we're so effective, frankly, it's been easier to win money." As a result, the pressure on Defence to get it right has been less. Defence carries a massive inventory and a large staff. Smith says modern management theory would say much of this is redundant. But this is the nature of a defence organisation and the sort of problems the Australian Defence department faces are common to pretty well all defence organisations. "It's interesting how much sympathy we have for each other," he says.

Smith rejects the suggestion that Defence administration should be cut. "That's not what the service people would say," he says. "Secondly, there has already been a massive reduction in civilian staff." At the end of the 1980s there were 40,000. Now there are a bit under 18,000. Part of this reduction is due to the selling off of the Defence industries and outsourcing. Smith says deployments of military personnel puts more strain on the administration. When the forces are not deployed overseas on operations – as was the case for most of the time between 1972 and 1999 – the services personnel for all three services undertake many administrative and policy jobs and work in intelligence jobs.

"We've had 60,000 or more ADF people deployed over the last six years and that's where they've come out. One of my groups is 150 or so people short because those jobs traditionally were filled by military personnel who are now deployed." Smith avoids calling for increased staff and says he is not personally persuaded that all staff are where they are most needed. But he says getting people out of the less critical areas into the more critical areas is a long process. "There are some areas where they are certainly under a great deal of stress. Operational tempo has been high for six years and it tells not only in the services but across the civilian support areas as well. But I think there's still a bit more we can do to make sure that people are where they need to be and that they're doing work that is necessary, rather than work that they've always done. That's the pressure I put on the chiefs and the group heads in regards to civilian staff. Don't just recruit someone new, or don't think you need someone new just because there's a new task. Go back constantly to what they're doing."

Smith says many Defence contracts come in on time and on budget and much of the criticism they wear relates to legacy projects. Project management from the beginning of the 1990s, where some of these projects originate, was quite different from what it is now. Secondly, he says what are often said to be cost overruns are due to comparisons being made with the figure quoted when the project was first mentioned. These were not necessarily overruns. The true comparison should be made with the price when the contract was signed. There were relatively few of these.

On the question of whether the product delivered what was promised, he says few come in with "diminished capability". "The areas that are most vulnerable … are anything with what I call the 'i' word in it," he says. "Anything to do with systems integration – we always seem to overestimate what can be done." He points out that Defence doesn't actually build ships or submarines or integrate things. It pays other people to do so "and sometimes we're too naïve in accepting what they tell us is possible."

This article was first published in the Canberra Times on 12 December 2005

The Man with a 'Promising Past' – Michael L'Estrange, Department of Foreign Affairs and Trade

The position of Secretary of the Department of Foreign Affairs and Trade is unusual in the bureaucracy in that the occupant is directly answerable to two very senior ministers – the Minister for Foreign Affairs and the Minister for Trade. The ministers are inevitably Cabinet ministers and with the Coalition in Government, it is frequently the case that one of them is also the Deputy Prime Minister. So it is for Michael L'Estrange, who must respond to the Minister for Foreign Affairs, Alexander Downer, and the Leader of the National Party, Deputy Prime Minister and Minister for Trade, Mark Vaile.

"We (the DFAT Executive) try to meet once a week, if not more, with both our ministers and parliamentary secretaries," he says. If Parliament is sitting, there tends to be more time over at Parliament House. L'Estrange starts his day with a run to clear his head at about 6.30 in the morning and then listen to the news. By about 8 o'clock he is in the office where, for the rest of the day, he is bombarded with a constant flow of information from all corners of the world. "Being the kind of service we are, a lot of our work is done overnight because we're operating round the world," he says. "I read the main cables that have come in overnight, the main issues in relation to policy and personnel issues and then we (senior executives) have a media meeting at 9 o'clock just to find out what is going on."

L'Estrange faces more than his fair share of meetings. In addition to the normal policy ones that any department head must deal with he meets with incoming ambassadors or those who are leaving. "I tend to meet all of them as they arrive and all of them as they leave and a lot of them in between, who come and see me about various issues," he says. I see all of our ambassadors before they go to their posts and when they come back from their posts. And when they come back in the middle of their posts. I also obviously have to be accountable for the administration of this department. It's a significant department, about 2000 Australia-based people, about 500 overseas at any one time, about 1400 or so locally engaged staff overseas and about 88 missions overseas." The department may not be huge by corporate standards but it is complex and when state and overseas operations are considered it operates at about 100 sites in about 80 countries where it is subject to the local laws.

L'Estrange says he has not changed the processes in the department since he took over last year. "I inherited a department that worked extremely well," he says. "I've got a lot of issues on my plate but re-creating the way the department works is not one of them because it actually works extremely well."

The interview for this article was conducted on the day it was first alleged at the Cole Inquiry into the oil-for-food scandal that DFAT was aware of kickbacks paid to the Saddam Hussein regime and the day after it was revealed that Australia's ambassador in Washington, Michael Thawley, had assured US senators that the wheat deal did not involve kickbacks. However, it was agreed that the interview would not canvass these current issues.

The first big challenge for the department L'Estrange nominates is counter terrorism, addressing the threat of global terrorism, not just in the high profile operations in Afghanistan and Iraq but also in the region. Counter proliferation of armaments is also a big concern, particularly in relation to weapons of mass destruction but also in relation to the illegal movement of small arms. "We're doing work through the UN and bi-laterally to try and reduce the level of arms. We're very focussed obviously on what is happening in terms of the relationship between the great and emerging powers in our part of the world, particularly the US, China and Japan, and what that means for us. With all of those countries we have important relationships so that's a big focus for us. Another big focus is our own relationship with regional and neighbouring countries. I think in this context we have a greater opportunity to do good things than we've had for a long, long time, particularly with countries like Indonesia, Malaysia and other countries of ASEAN and the Pacific Island countries. In that latter context we had some big resource involvement in PNG, including the Enhanced Cooperation Program and in the Solomon Islands."

The other big things he says they are focussed on are trade issues including the DOHA Round of multilateral free trade negotiation. Regional institutions also are on the agenda. Australia is hosting APEC next year and has just been involved in the first East Asia Summit. L'Estrange says these are very important organisations for Australia to be involved with. "We are a country which has its priorities in the Asia/Pacific region but we've got global interests", he says. "So therefore we're very involved in what's happening in terms of European policy; very involved and interested in what's happening in the Middle East, very involved and active in issues like climate change."

The final big issue he nominates is the security of Australians overseas, the missions overseas and the people who work in them, and the security of Australians generally. This involves the department in such this things as travel advisories, the new passport system and consular support for Australians in trouble overseas in incidents from bombs to bus crashes. L'Estrange has no career disaster stories to tell, or if he does he will not reveal them.

He remembers the first time he was sent across from PM&C to note-take for Prime Minister Malcolm Fraser at a meeting of a visiting delegation from overseas.

He was told how to get to the Prime Minister's office in the rabbit warren old Parliament House and did not want to admit that he did not know the geography. But he could not find the office. "I remember it was about 100 degrees and I was sweating profusely, marginally late when I finally found the Prime Minister's office," he says. "Thankfully the delegation was late. I remember sitting in that office thinking that this was not the way to make an impression on the Prime Minister. I don't think he noticed."

Today there is more to record keeping than note-taking and he says technology has complicated processes. "When I first joined the public service it was very much a paper dominated communications system – paper based and recorded and I think quite methodical. Now there are so many ways of communicating, electronic, telephone etc. Keeping a good track of all of this, as well as your normal cable networks and other things is a real challenge. It's a big burden and we are very much focussed on this at the moment. We've tried to address this in terms of making improvements. But technology keeps advancing on us, blackberries and everything else."

Whether emails should be kept on hard copy files depends on the email, he says. Some are chatty and personal. "I think if you kept all of them you'd have buildings all round Canberra to look after. "I think people should be keeping more … you can actually tell the 10 or 15 per cent that don't matter. But you're never quite sure of the rest. I think we have to err on the side of caution." DFAT was addressing the email issue and insisted that people as much as possible kept to the formal channels of communications.

L'Estrange says he knows how difficult it can be to be in junior positions and says this is one of the reasons why he is very sensitive to younger people today. "I remember 25 years ago walking into a big department and even though you've done a lot of academic work, it's quite imposing," he says. "I remember from those days people like Sir Geoffrey Yeend, Ashton Calvert, Sandy Hollway. They made a big impression on me because they actually made my role feel relevant to the big things that were going on … I do remember as a junior officer going to an inter-departmental committee at a time when whole of government was less in the public profile than it is now and turf wars were fairly strong. I was still fairly young, and given that people had been working on these technical issues for 20 years, it is quite an inhibiting thing when you put your head up and it gets chopped off and you feel a little bit reticent. So I always am very mindful of people coming into this department to make them feel that they're part of this machine."

L'Estrange says he is enjoying the job. "It is relentless and unpredictable to an extent because you are reacting to events. But at the same time there are these very clear interests that the Government wants to pursue in the long term. Some of them [like] counter terrorism and what's happening in our region and consular are big on-going issues. But there are the ones that hit you from the side ... and we have to respond to them. It's dynamic and it's very, very challenging ... I feel I've come through a road less travelled ... to get here than other people interviewed [for this series]. But I've got no less a commitment to public service in the broad concept of the term and I've been involved with it one way or another for a long period of time. And I really enjoy the opportunity of getting back into it."

L'Estrange did not rush into his career. After an extended period of study at Sydney and Oxford universities he joined the Department of the Prime Minister and Cabinet in Canberra in his late twenties. "You're a man with a promising past," an acquaintance told him after he returned from his stint at Oxford. "I always remembered that and thought I should make something of the future rather than the past," he says.

Today he is very much a man of the present and the future. In the media, L'Estrange has been presented as a political appointee to the position of head of the Department of Foreign Affairs and Trade. He is described as "a close political ally and confidant" of the Prime Minister, John Howard, or as a Liberal Party insider and conservative intellectual. There is no question that L'Estrange has political connections and work experience. He was executive director of the conservative think tank, the Menzies Research Centre in 1995-96 and earlier worked as a senior policy advisor to Liberal Opposition leaders Andrew Peacock and John Hewson.

But while he did not take the usual diplomatic route to the top of DFAT, looking back over his career and training, few can dispute that his experience has prepared him well for the position. In PM&C in 1981 he worked in the International Division on foreign policy. After a period with the Hope Royal Commission into the Security and Intelligence Services, he won a Harkness Scholarship to Georgetown University, where his supervisor was none other than Madeleine Albright, later to become Ambassador to the United Nations and US Secretary of State.

From 1996 to 2000 he was Secretary to Cabinet and Head of the Cabinet Policy Unit, where it is said he cemented his close relationship with the Prime Minister. Certainly the term as head of the Unit did him no harm, leading to his appointment as Australian High Commissioner to the United Kingdom from 2000 to 2005.

The son of a Sydney GP and one of seven children who attended St Aloysius College, Milson's Point, L'Estrange and his wife Jane have five boys aged from 12 to 20. There are pressures managing the work/family balance, he says, but "it's not as bad as a lot of other people and it's part of the job ... it's quite a good discipline, otherwise I think if you wanted to, you could work 15 hours a day seven days a week and not do the things you want to do. So you've got to prioritise and you've got to put aside time for them."

In the mid-1970s, just after John and Janette Howard had got married, they moved into a unit in Wolstonecraft next door to the L'Estranges. The young Michael knew Howard as the local member of Parliament and his father shared Howard's interest in cricket and the politics of the day. Did this make a difference in Canberra? "I knew John Howard in that context, but not particularly well," he says. Today the two are often described as having a close relationship of which L'Estrange only says has "gone on for a long time". "I worked for him for four and a half years employed by him as Secretary to Cabinet and then four and a half years in London where, because of the course of events and what was happening in the world, he visited London a lot."

L'Estrange points out that he has been working on public policy issues from his early days. His role as Secretary to Cabinet from 1996 to 2000 exposed him to a genuinely whole of government approach, not just foreign policy or trade. He says that since taking up the position of Secretary of the department he has not had any sense that he was considered an outsider. "Last year went remarkably smoothly in terms of working relationships. Although not formally an officer of the department, I was in and around it a lot over the years. In PM&C I spent all of my time working on foreign policy related issues. Certainly when I was Secretary to the Cabinet for four and a half years I had a lot of contact, directly, with the department. And obviously when I was in London for four and a half years I had an enormous amount of contact with the department. I knew most, if not all the senior people. I knew a lot of the middle people. So I don't think I was an unknown quantity. I've never felt an outsider and I don't think people perceive me as such because I believe in what the department works for. I respect the quality of the people we attract and I certainly strongly support the work they do in a lot of difficult places around the world."

In response to questions about his career and experience L'Estrange is reticent. He does not volunteer any juicy stories from his time in the Opposition leaders' offices or with the Cabinet Unit and even plays down one of the better, previously reported stories. It was said that after the Prime Minister created the new position of Cabinet Secretary and appointed L'Estrange to head it, the then Secretary of the Department of the Prime Minister and Cabinet, Max Moore-Wilton, asked the Unit to pay for its space in the department's offices in Barton. L'Estrange proceeded to find new accommodation – next to the Cabinet room in Parliament House and across the corridor from Howard's suite in the House. "That's just a complete beat up," L'Estrange says today.

Was Max Moore-Wilton bothered by the creation of L'Estrange's Cabinet Secretary role? "No. Not at all. In fact it worked extremely well. It does depend on personalities, I think, and it was a change. I think if you asked around for those four and a half years it worked incredibly smoothly and he was not just a close working colleague, he's remained a good friend."

L'Estrange says Moore-Wilton is "a colourful and very effective character" and, in the period he was head of the Prime Minister's department, he was extraordinarily effective. "You know the first year it was important that, as this was a new situation in that the Secretary of Cabinet, for the first time, was not the head of the Department of the Prime Minister and Cabinet, I think it was very important in the first year that there be a physical connection between the new Cabinet Policy Unit and the department. It was a new government and I think it established important linkages into the department on the ground."

As for the quality of their relationship, L'Estrange goes on to say, "I had a very close working relationship with him and I had a very good friendship with him and still do. So there's no sort of stories of bust-ups or wars there. We both respected that we had different kinds of roles although they intersected a lot. I was dealing with a lot of people in the department and I think it worked extremely well. So there was nothing really in that relationship that was difficult or strained."

L'Estrange says his time working on secondment in Opposition leaders' offices exposed him to the public policy process in a very direct way. Asked if people who take such positions pay a price when they come back to the public service, he says, "I don't think so." There are ways for people looking for a long term career in the public service to approach such jobs. "There are ways of doing them," he says. "Some jobs are more highly politicised than others in ministerial offices. People who are seconded from the public service tend to work on public policy issues in those offices which was my focus. I think most people do it that way so if they want to come back and accept the apolitical nature of the public service it's something they can do. So I think it's a matter of having an eye to the future as well as the present in terms of the way it pans out."

Asked if it makes a difference working in Parliament House for someone in Opposition rather than the Government he says, "Well I think it's obviously different because one is the Government and (it) and the public service are very closely aligned. But I think in terms of experience of the process – the parliamentary process and the public policy process – I think we certainly accept there's a place for that."

If there were any good lessons for the future from his experiences in the offices of Andrew Peacock or John Hewson, L'Estrange won't recount them. "I can't think of any one thing or anything in particular", he says . "But I think what I got out of it all was a much better understanding of the processes of the Parliament and the way the committee systems work and the way public policy evolves in terms of responsiveness to interest groups and I think in terms of serving the public interest it can be a very productive way to go."

L'Estrange was in Peacock's office during the 1990 election where he say he played "very much" a policy role. "I do think … people from the public service who are seconded tend to focus very heavily on the policy side of things and I think they can make the transition back." While he thinks the public service is essentially a career service he says there will always be an element of lateral recruitment and this is a good thing. "It's quite old thinking to think that the only people who can contribute to public policy development are people who have spent a lifetime in the public service. They do make a very important contribution. But others can make a contribution as well. I think it's right to be a career service. It will remain a career service. But not exclusively."

On the issue of the impact of the increase in political staff in the offices in Parliament House he says that as far as his department is concerned it has not really changed the nature of the interaction with the ministers. "[W]e provide our advice to the Government in terms of how to get where it wants to go in terms of policy," he says. "There are all sorts of ways in which that can be done. That's what we're about. We're about making this place administratively efficient and capable. We're about making it dynamic in terms of policy advice, but within the very clear context of where the Government wants to go."

L'Estrange noted that DFAT contributes ideas and perspectives relevant to the Government's determination of its specific policy priorities. But once those priorities are specified, DFAT is focussed on effective and accountable implementation. "We don't contest an end of policy because the Government lays that down. We suggest ways in which the objective the Government wants to achieve can be advanced. I think that's the right and proper way to do it. Now the process of that advice is very clear and open and I don't think anything has changed in that over recent years and I think it's a very vibrant and open exchange."

This article was first published in the Canberra Times on 13 March 2006

Californian Dreamer – Lisa Paul, Department of Education, Science and Training

The biggest privilege in her career, Lisa Paul says, was to be able to lead the Commonwealth's domestic response to the Bali bombings in 2002. Overnight she pulled together a large group from her then department, the Department of Family and Community Services (FaCS), and other departments. They took on the huge range of issues from the immediate – the way the Government could help victims and their families – through to the long term.

She says she learnt a lot of lessons from the taskforce experience, including how to bring a very diverse team together to do something quite out of the box. Paul is keen to thank others for the success of the operation, saying, for example, that Centrelink was "fantastic at responding". "They had the call centre set up and we were assisting families to fly to Bali and to fly to hospitals around Australia within less than 24 hours." Paul herself was also considered to have done a first class job and was awarded a Public Service Medal for her work.

In her career, Paul says she has rarely said no to an opportunity, even if some of the offers have been "scary". "Change is always a scary thing," she says. "Any of the moves I've made from one organisation to another, you know I've been anxious about because I want to do a good job."

Paul must have done a good enough job because she has risen rapidly in the service to head the Department of Education, Science and Training. This rise is all the more surprising because Paul says she did not set out to be a public servant. "It was probably an accidental career," she says. "I came to Canberra from Adelaide to go to ANU and hadn't particularly intended to enter the public service. But everyone seemed to be sitting the exam so off I went and sat the exam in Canberra High School."

Paul did well and was taken in as a graduate, beginning a career that has focussed on the human services areas – health, welfare, family services, housing, homelessness and education. Her career has taken her into both the Federal and ACT arenas, with about half her time spent in each. She says when she joined the service 21 years ago she did not envisage rising to the top. "I was really lucky in having a fantastic supervisor as my very first supervisor in the public service and she excited me about being able to offer public service."

Given her relatively young age Paul could well be destined to be Australia's first female head of the Prime Minister's department, a suggestion she dismisses with laughter and the response that she's only been head of DEST for a year and she's terribly pleased to be in this department and would like to stay for a long time.

No secretary expresses more enthusiasm for a department than Paul does for DEST. "It's just so important for Australia," she says. "It's also a great place to work." She points proudly to the national award DEST has won for excellence in people management and says the department is not only a nice place to work because of what it does, but it is also a great place to work because the people are great.

In Education Paul says she has now joined the family business. "Both my parents were teachers … and my father was a school principal in California." A little known fact is that she was born and raised in the United States, "but you can't tell can you", she says laughing. "My family first moved to New Zealand for a year in I think '67, '68 when I was about seven or eight. My father got an opportunity to be a lecturer at a teachers college in Christchurch, and then to be a deputy head of a new teachers college in Adelaide. So I grew up in Adelaide, did an Arts Degree, starting in psychology and changing to an urban focus and ending up with a housing focus."

After her public service exam she joined the Housing Trust in the ACT Government, starting a personal passion about housing, public housing and homelessness. She says she likes to say to DEST staff how exciting it is to work in a place that touches the lives of every Australian in a positive way. The department is important to Australia's future because, for the country to remain globally competitive, its people will have to be as skilled and innovative as they can be. The people working in DEST's vocational and technical education area are fundamentally reforming the way training is delivered in Australia. "In the face of a booming economy we face considerable skills shortages and the Government's given us this great privilege of being able to try to solve these shortages. We're implementing a whole range of election commitments. We've fundamentally restructured the whole framework of the national training system. So a person in DEST, in that area at the moment, is not only implementing huge reform, but is probably learning a new job, as well."

So will this mean that in two or three years time Australia will have no skills shortage? "Yeah, that's our aim," she says. "That Australia can actually match up the need for skills with the skills that are available. That's exactly the aim. But that's only one part of the department. A feature of our work at the moment is that we have reform in every area. So, for example, we're trying to … drive more national consistency in schools, looking at an Australian certificate of education … looking at how literacy is taught, looking at how parents get information about how their children are going."

While the state governments deliver education services, Paul says DEST is the only entity that can actually make national change, albeit often with the necessary assistance of the states and territories. At the moment, for example, DEST is working on a common starting age for schools. Paul says parents would love this, especially if they moved inter-state. Currently the starting ages range from four to six and have a flow-on effect through the 12 years of school.

One of the major challenges in education policy is indigenous education. "We're implementing reforms which put Australian taxpayers' money where it's most needed, which is mainly in remote areas," she says. "We're also focussing on things that work." An example is the funding of parents to help indigenous students. In the past a set amount was provided without limitations. But DEST now targets the funds so that parents work in partnership with their schools to make a difference to the students' education. Benchmarking is part of the process to ensure that such things as literacy, school attendance and retention are actually improving.

Paul says internationally Australia is "way up there" on schooling and usually only second to a country like Finland. On a typical day, Paul says she would definitely do something about the issues concerning DEST people. She might meet to discuss a staff survey or current accommodation issues, or the next certified agreement. During a sitting week she may meet with the ministers or their staff several times a day. In a non-sitting week contact tends to be by phone. Meetings range over a wide area including such things as policy, current issues, the budget or estimates issues.

Paul says she is keen to understand the details of issues which are both urgent and important. "But at the same time I'm keen not to get in people's way." She delegates to her deputies and senior officers but believes in working on the "no-surprises principle". "So normally we would talk in advance about any issues of the day. Usually I would know when there's going to be contact (between the ministers and their offices and senior DEST staff) and the nature of the contact because not only may I want to have input, but I may want to be there too. It's a very collegiate senior team and we would normally talk through issues every day."

Paul says she has never had a period in her career when she has wanted to leave the service and says every supervisor she has had has been "fantastic". But then she adds that some have been pretty challenging. "Supervisors can be frustrating … if they won't make a decision," she says. "Or if they don't stay calm. I like to remain composed and make decisions calmly. She says she is happy to assist, if people ask, when decision making processes becomes bogged down." And do they do that? "Ah well, certainly over the years people have come to me, absolutely. And you try to unblock a situation."

She believes it is essential for the organisation to get the whole culture right. "It will never be good enough to try to work on a case by case basis even though of course you must do so, and must be available to listen to people and sort through problems with people. But if that's all you do it will never be enough. I tell our people that they need to do two things —one is to be able to describe the strategic direction of where you're going. But the other one is to genuinely care for your people. And you've got to back it up." She says people ask her where they should go with their career and she replies that if they can go somewhere where they can learn both from the content, and from their supervisor, then that is the ideal. "You know when you're in a situation where you're not learning, that can be really frustrating."

A normal working day for Paul often runs from 8 am to 7 or 8 pm. Like many other department heads she also comes into work on the weekends, and often works on both Saturday and Sunday. "But I hasten to say this is not something one is necessarily proud of," she says. "We all strive for work and family balance so I wouldn't advertise [this]." Paul says she is "absolutely strict with myself that I will not ring people after hours except in exceptional circumstances. I do not expect people to be here on weekends and after hours." But she concedes that like her, other people will always go the extra mile. She says she has heard secretaries thank people because they worked on a weekend, whereas what they should have thanked them for was the great job they did. "You've got to be very careful about what you reward. I'm keen to reward the job people do. Not the hours they work. If someone can get the job done in half the time and go home early, fantastic."

DEST rates its senior peoples' performance on two bases. One is business, and the other is leadership. "You can't get away with being a poor leader over time because the metrics will speak for themselves," Paul says. On her own leadership style she says a sense of humour is really important. "I like to see the humorous side of things. I like to enjoy what I do and I like our people here to enjoy their jobs. I believe there is a direct relationship between morale and productivity. So it's not just doing your job but enjoying it as well."

The department conducts 360 degree feedback to assess performance. It also conducts staff survey and manager level surveys to determine how senior people are going and how their organisational units are tracking. Stakeholder surveys are conducted outside the organisation to get the views of the department's main clients. At the moment Paul says all of the metrics are looking positive. In the staff survey, for example, on the question of staff engagement, which covers not only being happy but advocating DEST outside DEST, the department got a 37 per cent positive response against the public sector benchmark of 29 per cent. In the stakeholder survey DEST has gone from 83 per cent customer satisfaction to 85 per cent. "We're starting from a high base and moving up," Paul says.

But not all outside commentary has been favourable and there has been some criticism from aboriginal communities over the lack of consultation about proposals for a nuclear dump in the Northern Territory. Paul disputes these claims. "Our consultation has been quite intensive and we've had a team both from our science area and from our communication area up in the Northern Territory with really in-depth meetings and visits over quite a period of time with the communities around the three potential sites," she says. She adds that the key in all these things is information and that this shows that the dump is not as threatening as people fear.

This article was first published in the Canberra Times on 5 December 2005

The 'New' Old Broom – Andrew Metcalfe, Department of Immigration and Multicultural Affairs

Andrew Metcalfe was plucked from the Department of the Prime Minister and Cabinet to head the Immigration department last year at the height of its troubles over the wrongful detention, or deportation, of citizens. In PM&C Metcalfe had been responsible for advice on the hot issues of counter-terrorism, security, defence and intelligence and was being tipped for promotion in this area. But the crisis in Immigration changed all that. Metcalfe, who had a long association with Immigration going back to 1981, and had gone to PM&C to get wider experience, became the obvious choice to head the troubled department. Over his 25 year career he has had stints in Immigration's interstate and overseas offices, its legal branch and as a Deputy Secretary, as well as a period as chief of staff for the previous Minister for Immigration, Philip Ruddock.

Throughout last year, and on into this year, the department has had its many failings exposed in official inquiries. It has been accused of having a culture that is overly self-protective and defensive. Staff were said to lack training and understanding of the legislation covering their enforcement powers. Former Federal Police Commissioner, Mick Palmer, said in one of the reports into the department's activities that DIMIA, as it then was, operated without proper management oversight, with poor information systems and with no genuine quality assurance, or constraints on the exercise of its powers.

Given his long involvement with the department, what does Metcalfe say about his role in the problems and the part the Government and the minister played in their development? "I'd say that I think it's up to others to judge ultimately as to where culture comes from and what's good and what's bad," he says. "As far as I'm personally concerned, I've always sought to act in the most professional way I possibly can to ensure that the work we do is legally and properly supported. I'm legally trained and I've got a long history through the organisation. I've had a long history working in operational areas with clients, in Melbourne, Brisbane and Hong Kong in particular. And I'm very proud of the work that I was able to do in helping refugees and in helping migrants deal with some of those issues."

But did the Government and Minister Ruddock's policies play a part in the lack of balance in the department's activities? "No. I don't think so," he says. "The thing that Philip Ruddock was very strong about, and still is, is a word he uses – integrity. That is essentially that people who stick by the rules, and have an eligibility, should be given the easiest possible way through the process." As an example, he says, Ruddock introduced the electronic travel authority and revolutionised the way services were provided to clients. "The department through the last 10 years has faced some enormous challenges and clearly has got some things very, very wrong," Metcalfe says. "There's no getting away from that. And that's the starting point for where we are today."

As deputy secretary under Bill Farmer, between 1999 and 2002, Metcalfe says he had a very strong sense of an organisation often in crisis management mode. "Did I have a sense of the culture being not right? Not to the extent that events have now shown," he says. Metcalf adds that, as one individual, Farmer should not shoulder the blame alone: "there were a whole group of us responsible for running the department. I know Bill very well and it's anathema to suggest that he, or any of us, would for a moment tolerate or accept as reasonable some of the things that happened. So the question is: Were the management controls in place? And clearly there was a breakdown in management controls through the organisation, perhaps fuelled by the crisis mode we were in, the fact that the organisation was then incredibly stretched."

"Did I have a sense then of the negative aspects of culture? I hadn't. I had a sense of an organisation that was very focused on delivering in some very difficult areas where you have to constantly pay attention to culture and clearly events have shown that the organisation failed in some areas. A lot of my work now is about trying to make sure that that doesn't happen again."

Metcalfe draws attention to the can-do attitude of the department in the past and the way it responded to challenges such as the evacuation of the UN compound in East Timor, and the evacuation of the Kosavars in the late 1990s. He says the extraordinary pressure the organisation was under with boat arrivals in 2000-01 is well documented. "It's easy in hindsight to look back and say you should have had detention centres built and ready, and contracts in place, and workers available for an unforseen group of 4,000 people to arrive because the people smugglers chose to send them this particular way. But the reality of having to establish facilities wherever you possibly could, so that at least there was some ability to maintain border controls, and some ability to maintain health checking and processing of claims, and whatever, was an enormous task. It was at that time that some of these issues that we are now seeing had their seed sown – poor work, assumption cultures."

Metcalfe notes that Palmer talks a lot about an assumption culture, where something happened and assumptions were made about the event. He also notes the criticism of record keeping and says the department has recently published a report dealing with the difficulties thrown up by the transition from paper records to a hybrid of paper and electronic records. On this issue the department is not alone. In the case of Vivian Alvarez, an Australian citizen who was wrongfully deported, Metcalfe says fragmented computer systems and poor record keeping contributed to the assumption culture. "Ultimately it wasn't a conspiracy," he says. "It was a series of stuff-ups that led one thing to another." What was concerning was that nothing was done when it became known within parts of the department that Ms Alvarez had been removed.

Since his appointment in July 2005 Metcalfe has shaken up the department. Three new deputy secretaries have been appointed – two from outside the department – and 16 of the 37 senior executive service branch heads are from outside the department. A change management process is underway and the Government has announced a $230 million package to redress problems. Metcalfe says this is not just about responding to problems in the detention and compliance part of the department. He says there are many positive stories to tell – the physical changes in detention, the health measures, the mental health strategies and the fact that women and children are now out of detention. The department is now trying to be "as open as we can". "We've got to be outward looking. We've got to engage with our critics, with commentators, with people who have an interest in what we do. And we are doing that all the time."

Some critics say the Immigration Act itself is too complicated and needs reform. Metcalfe, who has been working closely with the Act and its regulations since 1981, agrees it is complicated. "It's grown from I think 66 sections in 1981 to well over 500 sections now," he says. "I think there were 19 Migration Regulations in 1981. There are now volumes of them." The growth is a direct result of the changes in administrative law in Australia. Up until 1989 the two key provisions in the Migration Act were Section 6 which said, "The Minister may grant a person a visa" and Section 11 which said, "The Minister may grant a person an entry permit". Those two sections have been replaced by about two metres of documents. Metcalfe says the reason for this is that as the system moved to merit review it became necessary to replace very broad discretions in a minister and his or her delegates, with rules. What was previously loosely described, turned into dozens of different visa classes with multiple criteria designed to try and foresee almost every possible human circumstance.

Would it be better to go back to discretion? Metcalfe says that would provide great flexibility but far less certainty of outcome. Successive Australian Governments had seen it as a key aspect of executive authority that they would determine the eligibility of who should migrate to Australia and who should get a visa to travel to Australia. "The way that that's achieved is ultimately through regulations which have the force of law," he says. Safety nets exist through the minister's intervention powers.

Metcalfe says we would all like a simpler system, and the minister has asked him how it might be made simpler. But he also observes that the system has become more complex because it is more contestable, because more people seek review, and because more lawyers are involved in pursuing matters through the courts on behalf of their clients. Metcalfe recalls that former minister Ian Macphee introduced *Section 6A*, the very small descriptive element into the legislation. This was designed to provide some guidance from the Parliament as to who would be able to stay in Australia on a permanent basis, after having come in on temporary basis. That was described as being a safety net for a very small number of people. Within a few years it had grown to 20,000 cases a year because it was opened up by successive judicial interpretations.

The explosion of administrative law has resulted in the department having over 3,000 matters in the courts at any one time. These are largely appeals about refugee decisions. In March there were 168 active matters before the Administrative Appeals Tribunal and 2952 matters before the courts. Last financial year the department spent $46.8 million on legal services, $37.7 million externally and $9.1million internally. Its legal division has around 158 staff. "It's a big industry," he says. "[W]e make millions of decisions every year. It's really important to get things right. It's important that people have the opportunity to have someone else look at them."

One of the key things Metcalfe says he has wanted to focus on is client service in the organisation. "At the end of the day we're here as an organisation that serves the Australian community. We serve the interests of all Australians through the administration of a balanced migration program, through multicultural policies, through citizenship and settlement policies. But we have a more immediate group of clients who are applicants for services of the department, whether they are interpreter services, or whether they're visas or whether it's citizenship or whatever ... we are working over time to try and act as if we're not a monopoly, to give people choice about how they access us, to open up the ways that people can contact us and ultimately to be respectful in the way we deal with people and to be fair and reasonable."

Metcalfe says Immigration has a very ambitious set of projects underway – not just in response to the Palmer Report. They are re-engineering the relationship between the state network and the national office and modernising the computer systems which have been the subject of deserved criticism. At this stage they think it would be too risky to junk all the old computer systems. "What we're looking at is preserving the existing systems but using modern technology to put over the top, and around it, a system that allows us to interrogate the systems as if they were one."

Metcalfe says he knows full well he is asking a great deal of his staff. "I'm asking them to keep the business running everyday, I'm asking them to commit to this major change agenda not just in specific areas associated with practices in the past but more broadly as to how we do our jobs," he says. He says the department cannot back away from the fact that it has been, and will continue to be, the subject of deserved criticism.

Interviewed on March 7, before the release of the Ombudsman's report into Mr T's wrongful detention, he said there would be more reports coming from the Ombudsman about cases of detention that had happened in the past where the department deserved serious criticism. These were largely cases where establishing identity was a major problem and in some cases where mental health issues were a problem. Metcalfe says he is open to comment and criticism and there have been healthy discussions in the organisation. As part of the feedback he has had the first staff survey conducted in Immigration for many years. "I have found over the years that you get a far better outcome when you have a bunch of people sitting around talking through the issue than when you have one person who says 'I know the answer and this is what we're going to do'."

The impact the Department of Immigration could have on people's lives was driven home to Metcalfe early in his career. As a 28 year old acting state director in Melbourne in 1989 Metcalfe was thrown into the midst of a traumatic inter-country adoption case. The Immigration Minister is the guardian of children entering Australia under adoption orders. Routinely this power is delegated to the state child welfare authorities, so that the adoption authority in each state operates with the powers of a federal minister. In 1989 a young Indian girl came to Australia as part of the program and went to live with her adoptive parents in Melbourne.

One of the rules imposed by the Victorian child welfare authorities was that adoptive parents were to use contraceptive measures for at least a year following the adoption. In the particular case the couple had been trying to have a family for many years and had failed. At their first or second visit with the child welfare authorities the mother said, "I've got some wonderful news. You won't believe that I'm pregnant". At that stage the social worker said, "Oh, that's interesting. Let's just get the nursing sister to take the baby outside for a while and we'll have a talk about this." The woman was then reminded that she had been told to take contraceptives and, as a result of her pregnancy, the placement of the adopted baby would be reviewed.

In telling this story Metcalfe emphasises that these were state officials. A decision was made to take the child from the adoptive parents and place her into foster care with another family. That family were also on the inter-country adoption waiting list and claimed later that they were told that the child would be given to them for adoption. "The first we heard about it was when we were served with a writ," Metcalfe says. This sought to compel the minister, as guardian of the child, to produce the baby, take it from the second set of parents and return it to the first. Ultimately the minister, Robert Ray, decided that he would try and solve the problem by appointing an expert panel of eminent persons, including a senior department officer, to provide him with advice.

Metcalfe was involved in discussions with both families, the lawyers and the minister. The panel recommended, and Ray agreed, that the best interests of the child were served by its being returned to the first parents. The second set of parents reluctantly agreed. The minister's representative, Andrew Metcalfe, was assigned to collect the baby from the foster home. With two social workers, a male and a female, and with TV crews everywhere, they went in. "The family was surrounded by friends and supporters who were less than happy to see us … and I had to physically take the baby from the mother to secure its welfare and place it in the baby capsule. It was the most emotional experience I've had to that time." The media followed as he drove to the other side of Melbourne where he delivered the baby to "scenes of euphoria". "That drove home to me more than anything before, or since, how we are dealing with people's lives."

Metcalfe was born in Toowoomba in Queensland in 1959 and has a long family connection with the district. His father was a public servant, deputy head of the Commonwealth Employment Service in Toowoomba, and is well remembered for finding many people their first job. Attending Toowoomba Grammar School in the 70s, Metcalfe was appointed senior day-boy prefect, an unusual choice because he was not a sporting star and was not in the first XV or the first XI. He was, however, captain of the debating team, ran the school newspaper, and was dux of the school in 1976.

After studying arts-law in Brisbane, Metcalfe began his career as an administrative trainee in Canberra but with a girlfriend back in Brisbane studying law, he applied to a number of departments for a transfer back to Queensland and got a job in Immigration at the beginning of 1981. He rose rapidly in the state office and when his girlfriend and later wife, Jenny, completed her articles they returned to Canberra where Metcalfe took up the position of executive officer to department head, Bill McKinnon. In Brisbane Immigration, one of his jobs was liaison between federal members of Parliament and the department. "I recall one unpleasant experience where a very senior politician rang me personally – I was a very junior public servant – and told me in no uncertain terms what he thought of me and the department," he says.

Five minutes later he was phoned by the electorate secretary, very apologetic because the mistake in question had occurred in the MP's office. "That was the first time I realised there could be an unfair attack on you." Before he had received the second call, Metcalfe says he had walked in to the regional director virtually in tears to tell him what had happened. About 24 hours later the Member of Parliament rang and acknowledged he had got his facts wrong. He says the Brisbane incident taught him the lesson that you need to get your facts right before you go in. Metcalfe says he has probably in the past blasted someone and then realised he was wrong, although he cannot recall specific instances. "No-one's perfect and I'll say yes it has happened. I think it is rare. And I don't think it happens these days because I tend to be far more measured in what I do."

Metcalfe says he rose rapidly in the Brisbane office because he was there at the dawn of administrative law and he had studied law. Bill McKinnon heard about him and he transferred to Canberra. Not long after he came back an earlier application for a job in the Office of the Status of Women was successful and he joined it in the Department of the Prime Minister and Cabinet. The office headed by Anne Summers had at that time four men and 40 women, the reversal of usual public service balance of the day. Metcalfe says he found it fascinating. He co-ordinated the women's budget program, giving him an insight into the whole budget process across portfolios.

Promoted back to Immigration he headed the section looking after Freedom of Information and then moved to the legal branch to run the in-house legal advice and later the legislation section co-ordinating changes to the Act and regulations. After a period of consolidation he had a phone call from the then division head saying they had vacancies in Bangkok, Kuala Lumpur and Melbourne. "I said 'I'm interested but I'll have to talk to my wife ... I'll give you a call in the morning.' Jenny at this stage was a lawyer in AGS in Canberra. Neither of us had lived overseas. We thought that Bangkok sounded like a fascinating place for a couple of people in their mid twenties and the whole range of work, refugees, Indo-Chinese refugees and other things." Metcalfe rang back the next morning and said he'd like to go to Bangkok only to be told, "too late – you can go to Melbourne instead" where they lived for two years.

He then talked to the secretary about possibly going to Adelaide as state director but took another call from the division head responsible for placements asking if he would like to go to Hong Kong. "I said I was sort of thinking about Adelaide. Hong Kong wasn't quite in our thinking at that stage. We were starting to think about starting a family and so I said, 'Look I'm not sure. Let me talk with Jenny and I'll ring you back'. I rang Jenny ... and she said 'Ring him back and tell him we want to go!'"

So six weeks later, in September 1989, three months after Tiananmen Square, Metcalfe was in Hong Kong. Hong Kong had its eyes firmly fixed on the change of sovereignty scheduled for 1997. "From my point of view it was one of the best jobs I've ever done," he says. "It was a time when our office in Hong Kong, within the Consul General, grew from a medium sized post to our biggest overseas post. At one stage we had 14 Australian migration officers and 60 local staff. We produced more migrants out of Hong Kong in one quarter than out of the UK, the first time in Australia's history – business migrants, skilled migrants – just a fabulous group of people."

Metcalfe says many may have gone back to Hong Kong but there is a connection between the two places. In the four years he was in Hong Kong there were some difficult issues, working with people under a lot of stress. He returned to Canberra in May 1993, just after the election and was promoted to Assistant Secretary in legal branch where he had worked previously. For the next three years he worked closely with Dennis Richardson, later to head ASIO and now ambassador to Washington, supporting the changes Labor minister Nick Bolkus was making to the Migration Act.

Then came the 1996 election and Metcalfe's life changed again. He'd met Philip Ruddock on a couple of occasions when Ruddock as Opposition Immigration spokesman was in Hong Kong. After the 1996 election Ruddock made it known that if Metcalfe was available he would offer him the position of chief of staff in his office. "So," Metcalfe says, "in the time honoured way of many public servants I went and worked for the minister, for just over 18 months." In the office he was employed under the *Members of Parliament Staff Act*. But, he says, "I was a public servant before I went. And I was a public servant when I came back."

The period in Ruddock's office was one of significant change. Pauline Hanson had been elected to Parliament riding a wave of anti-Asian immigration and opposition to aboriginal welfare. Metcalfe says Ruddock played an important role in educating Australians about the reality of migration. "The lies that were being peddled about migrants ... were debunked by Ruddock and by [Deputy Prime Minister] Tim Fisher and by others." Metcalfe notes that the Government significantly reduced the immigration numbers in 1996, then adds that it has steadily increased the numbers over the last 10 years. "We've now got record number of migrants coming into Australia," he says.

This article was first published in the Canberra Times on 3 April 2006

The Company Man – Mark Paterson, Department of Industry, Tourism and Resources

Mark Paterson was an outsider when he was appointed head of the Department of Industry, Tourism and Resources four years ago. A former head of the Australian Chamber of Commerce and Industry, Paterson had no experience as a senior public servant. His brief stint in the public service in his younger days was in the state service in South Australia and ended in 1981, providing little training for the job of leading a major federal department.

On his first day in the job, Paterson called his leadership group together and asked them to fill out three pieces of paper. On the first they were asked to describe their relationships inside the portfolio, with other parts of government, and with organisations outside the service. This would provide Paterson with a relatively quick map of who the department dealt with. On the second piece he asked them to identify any key decisions that had to be taken by the executive in the next six months. And on the third he asked them to tell him what they would do if they were in his shoes.

Responses to the third request identified some unnecessary bureaucracy and unnecessary reporting in the department. Paterson's unconventional approach to handling the job was brought home to me when I emailed him seeking an interview for this article. An hour later I got a call, "Mark Paterson here. When do you want the interview?" I was a little taken aback: a Secretary who not only reads his own emails but one who makes his own telephone calls?

Paterson's lack of recent public service experience may well have proved an advantage in bringing about change in his department. As an outsider he had no reason to be bound by the conventional bureaucratic processes. "There used to be sub-committees of committees that met endlessly," he says. "But on examination I couldn't find that they'd actually produced anything. So we got rid of them. We didn't lose anything by doing that."

The department also got rid of a lot of the "wasteful unnecessary internal reporting". Paterson says he thinks coming from the private sector brought a different perspective to the task. "You're not steeped in all the traditions of the public service so you might approach things differently, in ways that people in the past either haven't done or have felt constrained by process from going down that path. I think we were able to ... approach change in ways that hadn't been done in the past." Because few people had come from the outside to the position of Secretary, there was little to prepare him for the task.

Paterson points out that there is now an Australian Public Service Commission publication setting out the key governance requirements for agency heads, but notes that such a resource "certainly wasn't available when I started". He says he had to be acutely aware of what he didn't know and what he needed to know. He says now the department does not have "an undue internal process, so I'm not constantly in internal meetings."

A key program managers' meeting is held every Monday, mapping out key strategic issues for the week and the major things that need to be delivered for government. The meeting invariably lasts less than an hour. "We don't need long meetings," he says. "We've cut down the notes that were prepared for that, to be sharp and succinct, so that we reduce the process time that stands behind it. "But ... it's a very useful forum, a very open forum. People come to it well prepared."

Every month they have a traffic lights report which tells them what is on track, slightly off track, or fundamentally off track. "We can see things that might be going off track and take remedial action, or if things have gone completely off track, we can start to work to get them back on track and decide whether we need to take alternative decisions."

Paterson did his university training part-time, gaining a Bachelor of Business from the South Australian Institute of Technology after study at four universities. "I moved from South Australia to NSW when I was part-way through my degree and I was confronted by the then inability of the Higher Education System to recognise one university's work at another," he says. At three of the universities he attended he was regarded as a non-degree student, but he managed to persuade the people back in Adelaide that what he'd done at the three universities was equivalent to the outstanding parts of his business degree.

Paterson's first full time experience was as a clerk in the Engineering and Water Supply Department in South Australia. He moved to the then Public Service Board. The early part of his career was in industrial relations and human resources related activities. Paterson left South Australia in 1981, moving to Sydney where he worked for the Australian Medical Association as a federal industrial officer. From there he went to the Chamber of Manufacturers of NSW in a variety of roles, consulting, and then on to the Retail Traders Association in NSW. In 1996 he came to Canberra when he was appointed chief executive of the Australian Chamber of Commerce and Industry.

Paterson says there are certainly substantial barriers to people from outside coming into senior positions in the public service. "I was an active investor and a reasonably active trader and I had to very quickly fundamentally change all of my financial arrangements because really in the nature of this portfolio I couldn't be a direct holder of shares in anything, because there was always the potential of conflict," he says. "I had to very quickly re-arrange all of the financial affairs, not just of myself but of my wife as well. So that was a very significant shift, unfortunately probably also, a very expensive one."

Paterson says that on his first day he was aware that people might have said, "Who is this bloke? Or what's he been sent here to do?" "I made it quite clear that I didn't come with a particular slash and burn agenda. I believe in growing the best out of individuals and organisations and that was my commitment to them." Nevertheless the department undertook a significant adjustment, in both priorities and resource allocation and staff were cut. "I knew we had to reduce the staff numbers," Paterson says. "I wanted a strategy which enabled us to manage that process. I looked at what our turnover was. It was clear to me that if we managed it appropriately then we could make the right sort of adjustments and we did it without a single redundancy at the time.

Overall staff numbers were cut by about 10 per cent. "I was open with people about what we were going to do … I recognised that, knowing what was to happen, they wanted certainty. But I wanted to consult and make some priority decisions before we decided which course of action we would take." When the final decisions were taken, an all-staff meeting was called where Paterson and the executive presented their planning.

Paterson says today his job is to ensure that there is a key sense of strategic direction and to properly identify what the priorities are. "There are many good things that we could be doing, and many good things that people could urge us to do and governments might want us to do," he says. "But we've got limited resources. So we have to make key priority choices. One of my most important tasks is to make sure that we take the decisions of what we're going to do, and what we're not going to do and the Government understands that. You can't just constantly load new activities on to organisations and just expect that they'll do everything that they've always done … I think the mistake that we sometimes make is not deciding what we're not going to do."

Paterson is well aware of the interest groups that vie for government support. "Every dog is somebody's pet," he says. "Every bad bit of regulatory intervention has a champion behind it … it may be a dog, but someone cares for it, and nurtures it, and wants to keep it. And that's not necessarily in the best interests of trying to reduce red tape."

When Paterson was appointed secretary the Industry department was already in the process of managing the cut in protection of Australia's manufacturing industries. Today, with quotas gone and tariffs significantly reduced, some might argue that the department no longer has a role. Paterson says they still have two significant sectors, the textile, clothing and footwear sector, and the automotive sector – where they're continuing to lower tariff protection and assist adjustment. He says they're also doing a significant amount of work with the Defence department in demonstrating Australia's core capabilities to participate in global supply chains. For the joint strike fighter project, for example, they had a Team Australia approach to have Australian industry participating in global supply chains with US Defense contractors. "The industry feedback that I have is that that's been a very powerful program and has delivered real outcomes for Australia", he says. "We will be able to roll that model out in relation to other Defence acquisitions."

Broadly Paterson sees the department's role as playing its part in developing Australia's overall economic architecture and framework. "We don't go out and advocate significant interventions in the marketplace," he says. "I think one of our key roles is trying to make sure that we pull government back from its intervention in the marketplace, that we try and remove the barriers that government over time may have imposed, or that the regulatory system over time has imposed on business. "You eventually get to as light handed a regulatory structure as you can, while still meeting the expectations of the community."

Lifting what he sees as the current deadweight cost of regulation is one of the major challenges. Hanging on the back of a regulation, there is often someone trying to keep it in place. The regulation was imposed in the first place because someone wanted the Government to "fix this problem, overcome this challenge, address this market failure or support this sector".

Paterson acknowledges that there have been a host of investigations and reports into cutting red tape in the past. But he says he thinks now there is "a genuine momentum for change" and points to the taskforce led by the Chairman of the Productivity Commission, Gary Banks, and the work the Council of Australian Governments is doing in the area. This, he believes, will make substantial inroads. "It's difficult and I don't shy away from the fact that it's challenging to try and reduce the regulatory burden," he says. "If an HIH collapses people come to government and say, 'this must never happen again.' But is ramping up the regulatory impost on every business in that sector the right way to go? I think we've got to seriously question that. Sometimes it would be nice if we had the opportunity to say, 'well, you might want government to fix it, but is that really the best way for us to go?'"

He says it is not only federal regulation which must be tackled but state and local government regulation as well. His expectation is that the Banks' taskforce will go beyond the broad sweeping statements of the past and come up with specific regulations to be dismantled.

Shortly after his appointment, Paterson told a luncheon that there were people putting out their hands for serious amounts of money and they are "the most belligerent, obnoxious correspondents I have ever seen". "I did say that ... I stand by what I said at the time," he says. "But I don't see as much evidence of that now." He says he thinks many people in the private sector don't fully understand public policy and the process of public policy development. "That's obvious when you see people come to town," he says. "They argue invariably from a position of vested interest, or of their interest at least. And they don't think about how that links in with broader government policy, they don't think about the second and third round effects of what they might be advocating, which are some of the things that we need to do in providing advice to government. You can take what may be a simple proposition that somebody comes to town complaining about, but you've got to think about how does that fit more broadly and how does that fit in the architecture of the regulatory structures we have? Who's that likely to have a negative impact on?"

Paterson says his department's interest is the national interest. "I think having a relatively consistent philosophical approach to many of these issues helps guide us in the advice that we provide to government. So if we have a shared understanding within the portfolio of the broad parameters, then it means we can be providing consistent advice irrespective of who the person coming in from outside might be, and whatever their particular interests might be."

The department covers a wide range of industries from manufacturing to the booming resources and energy industries, and tourism. Paterson defends having a whole division devoted to the single service industry of tourism while, for example, the Manufacturing Division looks after the automotive, textile, clothing and footwear, aerospace and building industries and another two divisions look after all the policy issues of the major export earning resources, minerals and energy industries. "Yes, it's a service industry," he says. "But there's a whole series of components to it and no one group controls the chain, so you've got accommodation, you've got events, you got the variety of potential experiences that people have, you've got airline capacity ... there is a very strong argument to say that government should be involved in supporting the tourism industry because the individual businesses can't capture directly the value that might be spent on broad media and marketing campaigns in key offshore markets."

Asked if he thinks it is essential for Australia to have a car industry, he says, "I think there is a very strong level of support, both politically and within the community generally, for maintaining domestic manufacturing capacity. The component suppliers build core skills, you get critical mass. There are those who would argue that we've got a strong medical devices industry because of the engineering and design skills that support the automotive industry. So I think it goes beyond just the iconic, 'should we have a car industry?' to 'well what's the broader nature of the skills base, the industry capability that we want for defence purposes, for demonstrating capacity in a whole range of other areas?' New industries like medical devices are often the combination of some good science, some great engineering, some ICT technical capacity and how you blend that together, and some market pull, understanding what might be needed in the market."

The car industry, he says, continues to be challenged. "Clearly it was much easier for them to compete internationally when the dollar was below 50 US cents than now with a 47 per cent appreciation in the dollar from that low. It is much more challenging. There's globalising capacity. There's some real challenges for the head offices of some US based companies, two of which operate in Australia. Their legacy health care costs for former workers and existing workers in the US are very significant challenges for those businesses, so we need to work very actively, and government is working very actively to support both the manufacturers and particularly the component suppliers to help get them into global supply chains, in a way, not dissimilar to what we've done in the defence area."

Paterson nominates energy market reform as a department success story. "We might not have met everybody's expectations but I think, if you tested it in a historical sense, very major progress has been made in energy market reform," he says. "Energy is a critical component in any developing economy. It's particularly so where you've got energy exports in the way that we have. Our energy intensive exports are really important to us, so having much more efficient energy markets, much more transparent processes, competitive sources of supply, removing the regulatory burden that's been imposed by having state-based regulators across a whole range of areas, I think very significant progress has been made there."

He is also proud of the work with Defence, where the aim is to lower the transaction costs for a global prime contractor to deal with Australian companies. "If we want Australian companies to participate in those sorts of global supply chains, both in design and in manufacture, we've got to be able to demonstrate their capability," he says. "Quite often they can't do that on an isolated, company by company basis.

He says it is important the they are able bring the companies together to demonstrate their capabilities and lower their transaction costs. As a result of this action, companies have won contracts in the design phase and on-going contracts are expected in manufacture and the life support programs for projects.

Administratively the biggest thing that has gone wrong in Paterson's time with the department was the suspension of the core research and development support program, R&D Start. "I started on the Friday," he says. "That happened on the Monday." He says they had a complex grants programs which on an accruals basis could be managed over time but faced difficulties in staying in line with annual appropriations. "We have contracts that vary in dollar size, vary in duration from three to five years, and the actual spend rate is determined by the private sector person who's the recipient," he says.

The grant recipients had traditionally underspent and the department would then get criticised for not working the program hard enough. Before Paterson took up the job, the department had tried to recognise the historic slippage and factor that into the allocations that were being made. It "cranked the program up" but at the same time unforeseen, economic circumstances in the business community meant that many people brought forward their plans and increased their spending and therefore increased the demand they made on the program. It could not be kept open because the department would not have been able to fund it. So Paterson suspended it. "That was a particular challenge on day two and it took a while to work those issues through," he says. "We were criticised for having done it."

He says the experience highlights the challenge of managing multi-year contracts where the spending pattern is in the hands of other people, all doing legitimate things, while having annual appropriations on a cash basis and accrual accounting. With the wisdom of hindsight, could it have been handled better? "We recognised at the time when we examined it that we could have done some things better and we could have done some things earlier than we did," he says. "We've put in better processes to overcome that. We've changed the contractual terms. We've got better planning arrangements between us and the individual companies in terms of spending profiles. We've got greater profiles We've got greater flexibility in the new grants about how we make the payments and the timing of those payments. We didn't have that flexibility before and historically it hadn't been needed because historically these things had always underspent. It was when we got more active in terms of trying to get the program out there to overcome that underspend, and had a significant increase in spending patterns by the individual companies that, when aggregated, put us in a really difficult wedge."

Paterson is not overly concerned about Australia's falling self sufficiency in oil. "We're very rich in gas," he says. "We're very rich in uranium We're very rich in coal. We have hundreds of years of supply of those products. We're a net energy exporter." He says liquefied natural gas prices are influenced heavily by the price of oil in international markets. Some of our crude oil is heavier and gets exported into other markets while we buy some light sweet crude for petroleum manufacturing and import some petroleum predominantly from Singapore.

The Government has provided on-going strong support for further exploration. The departmental agency, Geoscience Australia, does a lot of pre-competitive geological work, which is then put out as part of acreage release by the department's Resources Division. There are also new tax treatments in frontier areas where people have not previously explored and where the pre-competitive geological data suggests there may be potential. Very significant private sector capital is going into drilling in deep water, in frontier areas with no guarantees of success. "Over time we've been more successful in finding gas than oil but I remain optimistic in relation to opportunities for us finding future oil," he says. But we're an open trading economy, so if we're short in one area, then we'll import that and export other things that we've got in abundance."

On the question of using more gas, he says much of Australia's gas is in the North West Shelf while demand is in the Eastern seaboard. "At the moment it's more efficient to export that gas to other markets and get a price in those markets that justifies the transportation costs and the extraction costs," he says. "There are other potential opportunities. There's a lot of talk in relation to the PNG pipeline, feeding into the eastern seaboard market, being able to underpin our gas stock on the eastern seaboard. Using LPG or CNG for transport fuels will depend on the economics over time and I think it ought to depend on the economics."

He says the Government has an excise regime that recognises environmental contributions that also recognise energy content. It also has a bio-fuels strategy where it is committed to achieve the target of 350 million litres of bio-fuels by 2010. "I think the work that we've done in recent times means that we're reasonably on track to meet that target."

Before his appointment the portfolio lost responsibility for the major science agencies of CSIRO, the Australian Nuclear Science and Technology Organisation and the Australian Institute of Marine Sciences when the decision was made to link them with the Education department rather than Industry. "I think you can run both arguments about location," Paterson says. "What we have to do is make sure there is active engagement between this portfolio and the DEST portfolio to make sure there isn't a disconnect between industry and the publicly funded science and innovation community."

He says he's worked very closely with the Secretary of DEST, Lisa Paul, to ensure that there are no silo barriers. He points out that when Industry lost science it also inherited the Office of Small Business from the Employment and Workplace Relations department and gained the Business Entry Point, as it was then called. This has now become part of the department's e-business division, which runs a very large transaction based website www.business.gov.au. This offers the 6,000 odd forms that the three levels of government require of business to get a licence, to start a business and to operate a business. The department is working on ways to can make that interaction a much more efficient.

Asked why, if he favours cutting red tape, there are 6,000 forms for business, he says, "We don't control all of those. Many of those are state and territory based forms." Later when musing on the department's future, he says, "I don't think that the portfolio will stay the same size and shape, constant over time. The nature of change in relation to tariff protection, moving away from that and other areas, we'll evolve over time. Once we've achieved substantial reduction in the regulatory burden, found ways to manage that 6000 forms in a much smarter way than is done at the present time, then we'll move on with other priorities."

This article was first published in the Canberra Times on 2 January 2006

Making the Best of It – Mark Sullivan, Department of Veterans' Affairs

"I remember the day Peter Shergold [the head of the Department of the Prime Minister and Cabinet] rang me," says Mark Sullivan. "He said, 'Mark, I've got two pieces of news for you.' I said, 'Yep.' He said, 'One's good, and one's okay.' I said, 'well give me the good news first.' 'Well the Prime Minister wishes you to be a Secretary for another four years.' And I said, 'well, that's very good news, Peter. What's the other news?' 'Well you're going to Veterans' Affairs.'"

Sullivan says there was a pause before Shergold said, "What do you think about that?" "I'll be excited by tomorrow," he replied. Mark Sullivan took the job as head of the Department of Veterans' Affairs after the 2004 election. Today he says he loves it. "It's a wonderful job." When Peter Shergold rang him he was head of the Department of Family and Community Services, a department that many might regard as higher in the public service hierarchy than Veterans' Affairs.

Sullivan says he asked Shergold if the proposed move was because of "an issue about me" and was told that that was not the case. He then rang a couple of his senior public service mates who had previously headed Veterans' Affairs to get their reactions to the proposal. Alan Hawke told him, "Sully, you'll love it" and Noel Tanzer, from a very different perspective said, "It's a job you'll like."

In the administrative orders that saw Sullivan moved to Veterans' Affairs', FaCS lost a number of its functions. Sullivan says it was a department that had grown enormously and was responsible for over 40 per cent of the Commonwealth Budget. "I think there is at one level a risk management issue about one department being responsible for that level of government expenditure," he says. "It had also expanded its programs around children dramatically. The family agenda was a very strong agenda of the Howard Government and FaCS accepted much of the responsibility for things like family tax benefits."

But most importantly, Sullivan points out it was required to manage both sides of the welfare equation: "a lot of people said that maybe the problem with FaCS was that at its heart it was a department that cared for those that needed caring for, and took that care role extremely importantly. And in doing that, it was possibly not driving the back-to-work agenda of participating as strongly. I don't agree with that. I think FaCS was driving, and understood the participation agenda. But I do accept that the breadth of the department was such that you were juggling a lot of things at one time."

He says they were planning for significant administrative orders changes in FaCS and had developed a number of options as to what might happen. "Many of them were around saying that the workforce agenda either had to come into FaCS, and FaCS would dispose of other things, or it had to leave FaCS. So the change of FaCS to me wasn't a huge surprise. I think to leave FaCS as being still the single biggest department of state in terms of the expenditure side of government, and with an agenda around families going right through to the aged, shows it's no loser. It's an adjustment which historically was going to happen."

The new head of FaCS, Jeff Harmer, said in an earlier interview that the department had previously spoken with more than one voice. Sullivan responds, "We know. We worked in FaCS on the basis that people did have a view that FaCS had many voices." He says they examined this issue but added, "it is difficult when you've got a very large groups of people looking after the particular issues of children in our society, child care assistance to families etc, etc. We had people looking after the needs of aged people in our society, income support for aged people. And we had people looking after that working age group, from the supporting parents of disability pensioners, through to the people on Newstart."

"There was a diversity of view in FaCS. I think it was heard out there that we had a diversity of view and sometimes it was read as being 'they don't know what they want'." But Sullivan maintains the executive of FaCS and his ministers of the time, Amanda Vanstone and Kay Paterson, knew how to balance the issues. He recognises that the central agencies and the Department of Employment and Workplace Relations (DEWR) were saying, "Well we hear different messages".

When it was suggested that it was easy for DEWR to have a pure message he said, "DEWR had a more single focus and I think they pursued that focus with a vigour you have when you have a narrow focus. Look, I think FaCS was doing the job quite well. But it did not surprise me at all when these administrative changes occurred. And no, I don't think it was a loss."

The beauty of Veterans' Affairs is that no one has any doubts about its role. Sullivan says his role there differs from that of other secretaries. "I'm the Secretary of the Department of Veterans' Affairs and we've been a department of state since the mid 70s. I'm also the President of the Repatriation Commission, which has been in existence since 1918. I'm also the chairman of the Military Rehabilitation and Compensation Commission, which has been in operation since 2004. So we're a three headed place."

The Repatriation Commission has a policy role covering the same territory as the department – compensation and care for veterans who have been afflicted by war. The department pays pensions for disabilities, income support pensions and takes care of veterans' health problems resulting from war. It also runs a veterans' drug system which is generally in line with the Pharmaceutical Benefits scheme although there are additional items on the veterans' list.

The new Military Rehabilitation Commission, which draws on outsiders, such as the head of Comcare, Barbara Bennett, and Major General Mark Evans, acts like a compensation broker for serving soldiers, airforce and navy personnel. Sullivan says the men and women of the armed forces are well cared for from enlistment to discharge. And if they're injured, particularly as a result of engagement in conflict, Veterans' Affairs then takes care of them and their needs from discharge, through, hopefully, to their very, very old age.

He says there is an interesting social partnership. The Repatriation Commission was established in 1918, one year after the formation of the Returned and Services League of Australia, which focussed on the needs of returning veterans. It was not long after that that Legacy, with its very firm commitment to the needs of those who were left behind by fallen soldiers, was established. "That is one of the longest sustaining social partnerships we have in this country. Government really looks after the pensions, the health … the big ticket items. The RSL, Legacy, and other organisations such as the War Widows Guild look after other needs." He says unlike many other departments, the stakeholder group for Veterans' Affairs is very clear and the relationship is extraordinarily close.

One of the big issues for the department is ageing. "Over half of our workload is around World War II veterans and widows and they are of course getting older" he says. "Their average age now is about 84. They're falling in number. Their health needs are changing. We're moving from surgical to medical procedures and what is required to keep someone in a home." Sullivan says it also has implications for the department because "we're going to get smaller."

Wars involving the mobilisation of hundreds of thousands of Australians were hopefully a thing of the past. Australia currently had fine services, with about 60,000 people engaged and being deployed regularly, but this compared with a million Australians deployed in World War II. "Our job, when the job from World War II is finished, is going to be a much smaller job. So we'll be a much smaller department. We will focus on what are the very real issues of the day and they're around mental illness in the serving and veteran population."

Sullivan says the impact of war is now much more mental than physical, with the issues of post traumatic stress disorder and anxiety and depression coming from people who have been exposed to things ordinary people would never be exposed to. "These issues are very real and we have to address them."

Sullivan says the majority of the department's health services clients in a few years time will be women. Widows will significantly out-number veterans. The department is also starting to see the emergence of the Army's decision to incorporate women into basically all its activities, joining what the Air Force and the Navy have done in the past. "We'll see the needs of the young women veterans emerge," he says.

Another issue for the department is keeping the value of the Gold Card right. "The Gold Card is extraordinarily important to veterans who say it is the Government's answer to its commitment to care for their health in the event that they are damaged in war . We have to make sure that when a veteran walks into a medical practitioner, or a spectacle maker, or an appliance maker or dentist, that that person will take the Gold Card and know that they're dealing with a veteran and say, 'Yes, I'll deal with this card and I'll provide the service for the charge that DVA makes'."

Sullivan says the Government attempts to keep the Gold Card price for services right, but "it's not what you'd call the top of the market price". "We're a price setter," he says. "We say this is the price we'll pay and we want you to take it. And what we run the risk of is someone saying, "Oh no, we won't take that price. I won't deal with veterans." While few doctors say this, Sullivan says there is noise about the price.

Another Veterans' Affairs issue which received national media coverage was the road and recreation work at Anzac Cove, Gallipoli. Sullivan says people quite understand what it takes to turn on an Anzac Day dawn service at Gallipoli. "We're in sovereign Turkey. That's the first principle people need to understand. This is Turkey, the country we invaded, who are permitting us to come back to commemorate what happened there to Australians and New Zealanders and Turks. It's on an area about the size of Bruce stadium, but with none of the infrastructure – no power, no gas, no nothing. And we prepare for 20,000 largely Australians and New Zealanders to come and commemorate at dawn, and then go through in the morning what happened to the Anzacs at that beach."

After the criticism of the way the road works were handled the head of the office of Australian War Graves, Air Vice Marshal Gary Beck was not re-appointed to the job. Sullivan noted that the conflict between Air Vice Marshal Beck and the minister, De-Anne Kelly, was played out publicly. He acknowledged the work of Air Vice Marshal Beck and said he expected an appointment of a new head of War Graves early in the new year. "He [Gary Beck] achieved some remarkable things," he said. "It was Gary who really did take the Anzac ceremony at Gallipoli from a couple of hundred people at an open air cemetery to thousands and thousands of people at the 90th anniversary at the commemoration site in Turkey. He's a man who should be judged on his full record, not on issues between him and the minister in recent times, even though, in saying that, I'm not saying the fault lay with the minister."

Sullivan says complaints about the department are few and "we probably get more bouquets than most departments. A lot of veterans write to us and say, 'Thank-you. You're doing a great job.'" The veterans regard the department as "our Veterans' Affairs department". "There is a huge ownership by the veterans of the department and support for this comes in the department's survey which reports 90 per cent of veterans saying they like the services provided."

Sullivan thinks a lot of public servants should try working outside the service now and again. "They'd realise how great a thing it is to work in the service," he says. Although he began his working career in the public service and is now back, Sullivan spent time in mid-career working for Wang, the multinational computer corporation. "I was a salesman with a fancy title," he says. "They had some very, very large accounts and there were some major issues running about those large accounts, so my job was to solve a few of those issues. I enjoyed it. But ..."

He nominates work satisfaction and the importance of the jobs as two factors favouring work in the service. "You can earn a lot of money out in the private sector but there are very few jobs that aren't very narrow. In the public sector it's not hard to get into a job which is very broad and which you'll enjoy."

Sullivan was studying economics and accounting at Sydney University when the Tax Office offered him a cadetship providing the luxury of finishing his university course on pay. He joined Tax after graduation in 1973 and was posted first to its Sydney office, then Parramatta and finally to Canberra. He moved to the Department of Social Security where he was promoted to the senior executive service in Sydney and then moved across to the Special Broadcasting Service heading their Corporate Affairs group. SBS was "very different".

The common link in the move was Ron Brown, the head of Social Security in Sydney who had moved to SBS and asked Sullivan to join him. Nick Shehadie, a former Lord Mayor of Sydney, who Sullivan had known for a long time said, "It's a good job. It's to abolish your own job". "I said that sounds a good job. So I went off to SBS for a couple of years," Sullivan says. The SBS experience had him questioning whether he wanted to be a public servant all his life, so he resigned and worked for Wang for a couple of years.

But the public service lured Sullivan back, this time to Immigration, where he stayed for a decade as division head and then deputy secretary. "I guess I was pivotal in purchasing the Port Hedland detention centre in about 1990 for the Department of Immigration," he said. He was also one of the senior people engaged in managing the first boat people arrivals in 1989/90. Initially the arrivals were Cambodian, Vietnamese and Chinese, with a few Sri Lankans.

Sullivan was among those in the department keen to negotiate an agreement with China for the return of non-refugee boat people. The Chinese, coming from South-East China and particularly the port of Beihai, were the first large scale movement of people to Australia since the Vietnam War. Sullivan says the Chinese Government had a fairly cumbersome process in place to return its citizens to China. "We realised that the objective had to be to stop the flow. If you stopped the flow, or got some returns, you could have an impact. So we embarked on quite a strategic relationship with the Chinese to get them to deal with us differently to what they dealt with anyone else. It was really around saying, 'if you take them back and you find them not to be Chinese citizens, we'll take them back again'. And we need to move it quickly."

Where there were claims of refugee status, the refugee processes had to be followed, but Sullivan says there were not many such claims. Most said they were told that if they came to Australia they'd get a job. The department was able, over a few years, to put in place a system that stopped the flow. "[That's] something I was quite proud of," he says. The detention centres in those days were typically in capital cities and largely for over-stayers picked up off the street.

With the arrival of the boat people, Sullivan says there was a need for large scale facilities in the North of Australia where people were coming in, and as a result, he negotiated the Port Hedland purchase. Asked whether the Immigration department went off the rails in more recent times, he says he thinks the nature of the problem changed. When they were negotiating with China in 1990 they had an objective which was "how can we facilitate return and stop the flow?" "I think you saw that return wasn't physically viable for a lot of the more recent arrivals from the Middle East. It was very difficult ... I think the department was faced with a lot of people, long term, volumes were high, and something clearly went wrong. I don't think you can pick a point in time and say, that's when it went wrong, or was it different people in charge? Or was it so and so? I don't think that was the case."

He says the inquiries into the Cornelia Rau detention and Vivian Alvarez deportation revealed two very difficult cases. Like the current head of the Department of the Prime Minister and Cabinet, Dr Peter Shergold, Sullivan had a term as the chief executive officer of the Aboriginal and Torres Strait Islander Commission. "This was probably the best and worst job I had in my life, all at the same time," he says. "You don't ever forget your time at ATSIC. It's a job that has highs and lows all in half an hour."

The process for Sullivan's appointment to ATSIC took over a year, because he says the Board was suspicious of him as the Government nominee. "I made no secret of the fact that until I joined ATSIC ... I'd never taken much of an interest in indigenous affairs and my aboriginal friends were nil. My aboriginal acquaintances I could count on one hand." The rewards from the job were that it gave a personal insight into aboriginal life, its rich heritage and traditions, and its languages and peoples. Sullivan says it provided many little instances that he would never forget.

"The frustration is the frustration for so many. You thought you'd see progress. You thought you would see change. And sometimes it would sustain. But so many times it was just frittered away. It was based on the shoulders of too few individuals in the community and if those individuals cracked under the pressure, a community could go backwards so fast ... the frustration was that our programs didn't fit what aboriginal communities and societies needed."

"I think the thing that Peter Shergold is leading in indigenous affairs, if it goes to its conclusion, will be the greatest thing that could possibly ever happen. The traditional government model is to say, we'll create programs, design programs, advertise them and you say whether you can fit. The new indigenous model is, you tell us what you need and tell us what result that will have in your community and it doesn't matter if it doesn't fit a program, we'll make that a program for your community."

During his time Sullivan at ATSIC there were number of national events including the Olympic Games, the Centenary of Federation and the end of the ten years of reconciliation. He says that when he took the job ATSIC had no relationship with the Government. "It seemed to me to be ridiculous for a government agency to have no relations with the Government. One of the things ... I was promoting within ATSIC was to say that differences with Government do not mean that you close down relationships."

"There was a term around at that stage – practical reconciliation. My advice to ATSIC, and they largely took it, was to say concentrate on practical reconciliation. You can maintain your policy objectives on a treaty or in respect of 'sorry' or other things but also be pragmatic and say that this Government is not going to suddenly say, 'we've changed our heart' or they're not going to say, 'yep let's have a treaty with the aboriginal peoples of Australia'. But you can work with them. So work with them, Peter Reith, [the then minister of Employment and Workplace Relations] on employment issues and work with the Prime Minister and work with other ministers."

This article was first published in the Canberra Times on 16 January 2006

Going 'Bush' – Joanna Hewitt, Department of Agriculture, Fisheries and Forestry

Times have changed dramatically since the early seventies when Joanna Hewitt was a trainee in the Department of Foreign Affairs. At that time regulations were regulations and far be it for anyone to think that a bit of commonsense should apply. If the overseas determination referred to "the officer and his wife", how could a married woman – even one recruited as a graduate foreign affairs trainee – be posted overseas? "Everything was driven by the Public Service Act," Hewitt says. "To go out on my first posting I had to wait a whole year longer than the other trainees because I was married. It took a year to have that wording changed to refer to 'his or her spouse'."

Recounting her experiences as a woman who has risen through the public service ranks to head the Department of Agriculture, Fisheries and Forestry, Hewitt is able to recall a number of instances when foolish rules blocked her path. Her first few years in the service followed a classic Foreign Affairs path – a posting to Stockholm in the mid-70s when everyone was fantastically interested in the Swedish economic model. But she left the service for thee years when her children were very young and moved interstate.

"When I came back [in 1983] I wasn't able to go back into Foreign Affairs. It had a fairly closed culture. It's changed dramatically since. But in those days the only way, as a graduate, you could enter foreign affairs was if you came in as a Foreign Affairs trainee. You weren't allowed to enter at any other point. They said, 'We'd love to have you back, but the only way you could come back is if you came in as a graduate again.' I remember speaking to the head of staffing who at that time was one of my fellow trainees from 1972 and he said, 'I'm really embarrassed about this Joanna but we can't do anything. It's the rules'." So Hewitt went briefly to the Office of National Assessments and then to the Prime Minister's department.

A few years later, Hewitt was promoted into the Department of Trade, and had just settled into the job when the Foreign Affairs and Trade departments were amalgamated, returning her to her first department. Today, department heads have huge discretion to overcome the sort of barriers Hewitt encountered.

The daughter of a bank manager, Hewitt went to school in rural Western Australia and Perth. She says she lived in nearly every little town in Western Australia and went to eight or nine schools. "I think most farmers probably see their local branch bank manager as a friendly face," she says. "I had friends at school who worked on farms. I spent a lot of time in shearing sheds and that sort of thing, at weekend stays with school friends and I have a sense of the countryside." She joined Foreign Affairs after completing an Economics degree, but later took time off and went to the London School of Economics to undertake a Masters degree.

Few issues have divided the Australian Government more over the last twenty years than the harvesting of native forests. In 1988 Hewitt was right in the thick of it, managing the land resources division of the then Department of Primary Industries and Energy, at the height of the conflict. "It was at a time when we, the Primary Industries department, and the Environment department were at loggerheads, echoed in spades by the fact that the then ministers, Cook and Richardson, were often completely at odds with each other," she says. "It was a very, very tough thing to do because the stakes were so high. There wasn't that sense of common purpose across government that is a hallmark of how we operate today."

Hewitt says it is a pleasure to come back to the department and to work with a colleague like David Borthwick, the current head of the Department of the Environment and Heritage, and to have a joint team working on a lot of the natural resource management issues in a very harmonious way. "It's not that we always have exactly the same set of priorities … but we're pretty close and where we can't reach agreement amongst ourselves we simply set out the differences in advice to ministers."

Of the past she says, "Oh, it was dreadful. Very high conflict, very narrow association of each portfolio with its stakeholders. Your own staff would see some terrible travesty, as we saw it, against good process or good evidence-based advice, being committed. You'd see some nonsense written down about something to do with the way the forest had been harvested, or the conservation values of a particular piece of forest, and the temptation was to fight fire with fire. I spent a whole year trying to really encourage my own staff not to match what they saw as an inappropriate way of going about the work with their own counter-balancing inappropriate behaviour."

The lesson Hewitt says she learned was how difficult it was to work well without the framework of good process. "If you don't employ good process to get the issues aired, articulated and decided, it's very, very difficult." If ministers are in serious conflict, the actions public servants can take are also limited. Today she says the catchphrase they use in her department is "evidence-based policy advice". This is why they have two specialist bureaus, the Bureau of Rural Science and the Bureau of Agriculture and Resource Economics. Policy people, who are much more caught up in the immediate, or the short to medium term, are able to draw on the bureaus' expertise.

The bureaus are not huge but "they've got some fantastically highly skilled and well regarded specialist scientists and economists and they make such a difference to the quality of what you can contribute to government". DAFF and the Environment department now operate a joint team, located in the DAFF offices, to manage natural resource programs and produce policy advice to ministers. Asked about the different policy perspectives of the two departments Hewitt says, "We don't take the view of ... the industry come hell or high water but we do make sure that we understand their view. We sit down and look at the evidence and take into account, and are mindful of, and informed about, the impact on the industry of the particular course of action."

She says the Government has quite clearly articulated priorities in the environmental and resource management field. The industry groups now embrace the idea that they need to preserve the resource base for the future of the sector and the next generation in farming. The Regional Forest agreements now in place mean that the lines have been largely drawn. Hewitt says part of the debate in the wider community about preservation of forests was about "aesthetics and landscape". "So whether a harvesting process could be sustainable in a technical sense, or not, is important but does not always settle a dispute. The Government has drawn its lines. Every now and then there's pressure to re-draw them, as we saw around Tasmania during the last election, and those issues have to be worked through and resolved. But there's a very professional and very civilised spirit in which that's done now." Government processes are clear "and that's much more rewarding than the old battles which became very personal".

Hewitt says she learnt a huge amount from the experience of the late 80s "but I wouldn't say I enjoyed that very much". After 18 months she told her then department head, Geoff Miller, she would like to do international work.

DAFF today is a big, very diverse organisation. As Secretary, Hewitt sees the most important part of her role as setting a direction and "pulling the bits together". The department has a clear mission focussed on the agriculture and food sectors, expressed officially as being to support the profitability, sustainability and competitiveness of the sectors. This is done in a variety of ways with specialist functions and scientific streams.

Two thirds of DAFF, in both money and people terms, is the Australian Quarantine and Inspection Service (AQIS) which has a significant presence in the regions. Specialist economic work is conducted by the Australian Bureau of Agriculture and Resource Economics which Hewitt describes as "a bit of a jewel in the crown". The department also conducts the standard functions of policy development and program delivery, with some quite large program activity. This includes spending on natural heritage, exceptional circumstances drought assistance and industry other programs.

Hewitt says DAFF has a huge number of external stakeholders. "When I came to the department from the Department of Foreign Affairs and Trade, I was quite struck by the intensity of the external contact," she says. "In DFAT the whole world is your external environment. But here, although the agriculture sector is quite modestly supported by the Government − very modestly by any international comparisons −there's a lot of connection between the sector and the business of government. The portfolio industries draw on statutory authorities to collect levies for their marketing and to collect levies for their research and development work, which the Government matches."

Although generally speaking government policy does not involve subsidises, much of the way in which policies are given effect requires government involvement. Hewitt nominates the competitiveness of the sector in the face of new global players in some industries like horticulture and management of bio-security as the priority challenges for the department. Agriculture, Forestry and Fisheries is responsible for nearly a quarter of Australia's exports. To underpin their competitiveness, Hewitt says the department must work with the industries to make sure that the Government sets the right business environment in the most effective way it can. "Partly that's undoing things, trying to reduce the regulatory burden and so on and partly it's in the external world," she says.

"There's a big contribution we can make on the trade side to win market access internationally. Agriculture is still one of the last areas where other governments have damaged the prospects for Australian producers in terms of market opportunities. Our terms of trade [the price of Australian exports relative to its imports] over the years have just kept falling so winning new markets is a way of offsetting lower real prices. That's slow hard work."

Hewitt says the department aims to make sure that research and development policies are also set effectively to help keep Australian producers ahead of the declining terms of trade. In the bio-security field she says it is undeniably the case that Australia has done pretty well in preserving its very favourable quarantine status. But there is now a lot more pressure, partly because of the huge increase in the movement of people and goods across the borders.

The department recently ran a trial to test Australia's preparedness for an avian influenza outbreak and Hewitt says they must be prepared for new disease or the re-emergence of some old ones, such as foot-and-mouth disease. Managing the bio-security challenge has to be done in a responsible manner, proportional to the risk. It should keep Australia's favourable pest and disease status, but can't be a "stop the world I want to get off" approach. "You can maintain a very low risk policy setting, but not zero, and that's a very challenging thing to communicate and to set right in policy terms," she says. "It's highly controversial. We get an awful lot of drama around issues as they arise."

In the year she has been in the job Hewitt has had the practical experience of managing work, across the jurisdictions, of a citrus canker outbreak in Queensland and the possibility that Australia might have had a disease affecting pigs. She says Australia faces pressure from trading partners wanting liberalisation of its quarantine regime and pressure from domestic industries who are anxious about disease status and sometimes import competition. The challenge is to get it right when there is pressure from all sides.

Reforming regulations is another area where Hewitt believes her department can play a useful role. She says that, for example, Australia is successfully exporting primary agriculture commodities and some processed items such as wine, but could do better in processed food export and domestic markets. "If you have very conservative settings in the food standards side of things, it's a disincentive for companies to innovate and to try new things," she says. But she acknowledges there are real public health and safety issues to be dealt with.

Another area that is topical and controversial is the moratorium all states, except Queensland, have on allowing the commercialisation of genetically modified canola crops. She says internationally a lot of Australia's competitors have made the move to use GM canola. There are commercial advantages from the productivity performance of the modified crop and "when we look at the international markets for canola we don't see any disincentive or price discrimination between GM and non-GM canola".

Asked to nominate the regulatory knot she would most like to untie, she says one of the most difficult is in food regulation. The difficulty reflects Australia's constitutional make-up, where state governments have the primary responsibility to take action. "You're pulling together all the jurisdictions, and the health and agriculture portfolios have an interest in the way the standards are set ... On the whole the Australian Government ... has wanted to see a bit more streamlining, a bit more flexibility introduced into the way the standards are set – not to take any risks with human health by any means, but to be able to move a little more quickly."

In her first year in the job, Hewitt has been preoccupied with the Government's response to the drought and the debate over the rationale for support. "We hope we're now moving to a more positive phase in the climate cycle," she says but then adds, "It's still a very big issue for us." She recalls that when she was Ambassador in Brussels arguing Australia's case against European agricultural subsidies, she tried to explain to people in the European Commission that in Australia, farmers did not even bother knocking on the door for drought relief until they had had two failed seasons in a row. The policy setting was that support kicked-in during an event that was one in 20 to 25 years and, by definition, this was not the sort of event that could easily be planned for.

She says there is more debate about the support that is provided on the business side, subsidising interest rates and support for farm enterprises. She points out that this is all done with assets and income tests and is strictly constrained. On the welfare side – the payments that keep food on the table and kids clothed and getting to school – support was only for a very limited period. "We've extended that period a bit in the last drought because it's such an exceptionally long one. I think the welfare support is completely accepted. The business support is more debated … we're doing some work now through the Primary Industries Ministerial Council to look for, and try to get a better consensus, on the detail of drought policy for the future – hopefully for the next event rather than the one we're just emerging from."

Hewitt says staff in her department feel a sense of affinity with the sector. "There's a tremendous sense of commitment to doing something important for the sector and for Australia," she says. "DAFF people have a real sense of rapport with people in rural Australia … I think there's a great sense of purpose about the job … people feel that they're doing something that really matters."

Overall, Hewitt's career path in Foreign Affairs and the Primary Industries departments provided her with the ideal background to undertake her current role. But she says she was "not a career planner". "I've always –with one exception – thoroughly enjoyed the work I've done and then something else has sort of presented itself and I've said, 'oh, that would be interesting', so I've gone on to it." She says she probably spent more of her career on trade issues but she has worked in three divisions in primary industry, the livestock and pastoral, the land resources and the corporate policy.

After she was promoted from Deputy Secretary in DFAT to head DAFF she says she had to establish the personal contacts to enable her to be able to pick up the phone and talk to the key people in industry, peak bodies, research and development corporations and elsewhere. Today, two of her children are in their twenties, living and working overseas. But she still has a 14-year-old son living at home. She is in the office by 8 am most mornings and tries to get out by 7 pm. At weekends she works from home. "I've got a terminal at home and we work on Blackberries quite a lot … it's been brilliant actually."

Because the portfolio has many stakeholders, she often has dinners to attend in the evening. "There's an endless number of invitations. I try quite hard to limit it to two, maximum three a week," she says. "I do very much encourage people to come and see me in the office if they can. But you do need to build up a certain rapport with industry and other people you're working with."

This article was first published in the Canberra Times on 26 December 2005

The People's Choice – Jeff Harmer, Department of Families, Community Services and Indigenous Affairs

Family and Community Services was the department that appeared to be the loser in the new administrative arrangements announced by the Prime Minister, Mr Howard, following the election in October 2004. Before the election the portfolio covered the major government payments agency, Centrelink, and the department itself had the Child Support Agency as a division. Following the election both these agencies were transferred to the newly created Human Services portfolio and Dr Jeff Harmer was transferred from the Department of Education, Science and Training to head the now smaller Department of Family and Community Services.

Harmer, as one would expect, takes a positive view of the changes. "As a newcomer in the department I didn't feel, as others may have, that we'd lost something," he says. "I actually think that the department in its new form makes very good sense and I was delighted to get it." He says there is no doubt the department is smaller. It has lost three of the income support payments for those of working age but has absorbed considerable functions from ATSIC and also gained the Office for Women from PM&C. "I think it's more cohesive now. The programs that we have are programs aimed at supporting those who need ongoing government assistance and community support."

Harmer says the department is still very large. It has responsibility for pensions and family payments, including child care, and it is a critically important department for the Australian community. "As the biggest spending department we run about a quarter of the budget. We are responsible in policy terms for over $45 billion. We have 80 programs and over 15,000 service providers and therefore have a huge footprint in Australian society reflected in our purpose of improving the lives of Australians."

Harmer says that when they were redesigning FaCS they spoke to stakeholders, who said that the older, larger FaCS did not always speak with one voice. "We are now determined that FaCS is much more integrated and speaks with one voice. We have one position on all the key issues and wherever you contact FaCS around Australia, you basically get the same position."

The sometimes contradictory positions arose from the fact that the old FaCS was trying to actively pursue Welfare to Work objectives while at the same time trying to support the most needy in society. "So when our stakeholders were dealing with FaCS on the one hand we were saying 'get out there and you've got to get to work'. And on the other we were saying, 'look, we want to help you, how can we help?' It's much less ambiguous now because we're much more like a traditional family and community services department."

Harmer says when stakeholders interact with FaCS across the country they will basically get the same story and services. "People don't give their own personal views as they may have been inclined to do before. They give a FaCS view – we call it 'One FaCS'. That's professionalism." Harmer says it is a family oriented department focussed on support and services for families, older people and those most in need. "It's a 'softer' department in some respects than it was before, because DEWR [the Department of Employment and Workplace Relations] now has responsibility for making sure that people on some welfare benefits are provided with the opportunity to get work rather than going on to payments."

To the suggestion that DEWR has been given the bastardry bit and FaCS has got the good guy work he says, "Well, I wouldn't put it that way. But they've certainly got the job of being tougher on eligibility for those payments because the priority is to get as many as possible into work. Our services are complementary." Harmer says staff in FaCS feel they have a responsibility to make a difference to the Australian community in areas such as income support for the aged, in family tax benefit and other family payments, childcare and early childhood, programs for housing, the homeless, for people with disabilities, youth, indigenous Australians and women.

The creation of the new Department of Human Services, which not only took responsibility for some of FaCS service delivery agencies, but was in part funded by money drawn from FaCS, has the potential for both overlap and conflict. But Harmer maintains the lines of responsibility are clear. He says Patricia Scott, the head of Human Services, is responsible for the efficient delivery of programs for a range of portfolios. But the policy making – the determination of where the money's spent, how it should be spent and who is eligible – is done in Family and Community Services and in the other policy departments of Education, Science and Training, DEWR and Health and Ageing. "Our minister has policy responsibility and Minister Hockey [the Minister for Human Services] has responsibility for delivery."

He rejects the suggestion that Human Services, as an accountability agency, might play a role in watching FaCS and says they are set up to oversee the delivery agencies, such as Centrelink. "[The Department of] Finance, their big brother, if you like, have responsibility for watching the way we allocate the resources and for keeping tabs on our expenditure, monitoring and putting the opposition case when proposals are put forward to spend money on a new program."

Human Services might put up suggestions for more efficient delivery. FaCS would listen to Human Services where their experience in running the delivery arm meant they had some information that might be helpful for policy development. Harmer says they have had lots of debates with the Department of Finance. "Quite often it's a misunderstanding that happens which can be cleared up quickly," he says. "I from time to time speak with Ian Watt [the Head of Finance] when I'm unhappy with a co-ordination comment or unhappy with a position they're taking or something. Or he might ring me because he's unhappy that we let them down on a deadline. I regard that as an important element of my job. And I'm usually able to quickly resolve the issue. Sometimes we agree to disagree and ministers go into Cabinet with different points of view. It's an inevitable part of the democratic process."

Harmer previously headed DEST which he says is a very strong department. One of the big challenges following the machinery of government changes, he says, is to re-build FaCS. "I've put a lot of personal effort, as have my senior managers, into re-organising Family and Community Services, restructuring it, placing some new people in key roles and giving it a new purpose, a new direction," he says. "We've invested heavily in what we call our core business processes, a key strategy to manage risk, support staff and to ensure that we don't 'drop the ball' in some areas that are basic to our success."

So what is basic to success? "Policy advising, implementing programs, managing issues, managing stakeholders and financial management and governance," he says. "There are five of them and we put a lot of effort into specifying what they are and documenting them. We are also making sure we have a 'one FaCS' view of all five so that wherever you are in Family and Community Services you know how FaCS does policy advising, you know how we do program implementation and so on."

FaCS is currently looking at how it can simplify the way it does business with its service providers by reducing unnecessary red tape while maintaining appropriate standards of accountability and transparency for government. Harmer says they run 80 programs and some of the big service providers interact with the department across ten or more programs. "Because the programs have been developed at different points in time with different people involved, the requirements on the service providers to apply for funding, furnish financial acquittals and provide performance data, are quite different. For example, Anglicare, who deal with us across many programs, or Catholic Welfare or a range of others, get frustrated about having to fill in different forms for different programs. The minister is very active in driving this agenda." He says he thinks they can rationalise the processes and streamline some of the requirements.

On policy advising he sets out a clear process. "We don't start from picking up a piece of paper and starting to write. Policy advising is really about understanding the policy context, understanding where government is coming from, what their parameters are, what will fit with the Government's philosophy and agenda. You have to have some understanding of that before you can be successful in advising Government in policy. That doesn't mean that you give ministers what you think they want to hear. But it does mean that you'd better know the framework ministers will use to evaluate your policy advice if you hope to be successful in influencing them. That's a really important first step which is mandatory. I want everyone in Family and Community Services who is in the policy advising business, to first of all understand what the Government's philosophy and Government's policy is. New staff are told to talk to their senior people and will be given background papers to read. You need a starting point for your policy advising role, rather than thinking of it in a purely academic framework."

Reading between the lines it appears that Harmer has had trouble with those advocating personal views. "I'm interested in your professional views and your professional views about policy come from your understanding of Government priorities, combined with all the evidence and information available to you. When people come to Family and Community Services they come to be professional public servants, not to be advocates. I'm not after advocates for particular points of view. I'm after people who are professionally giving advice according to the evidence and against the background of the Government's policy agenda. Then the issue is how to write it up and make it digestible. You can't write a huge research paper and expect you minister to read all of it. You've got to think about how to succinctly write it, how to frame options, how to argue the case – the pros and cons to make it digestible for the minister. You need to give them all the information, you need to give them options and it's a responsibility of a FaCS officer to make a recommendation on the basis of all the evidence and the advice. The minister will then either choose to take it, or not."

Harmer moved around a lot in his 28 years in the public service before taking over FaCS. Starting off in Environment, Housing and Community Development in 1978 he moved through various agencies including Finance, Social Security, Housing and Construction, Community Services and Health and Housing and Regional Development. His appointment as Secretary of FaCS was his third as an agency head having previously led the Health Insurance Commission between 1998 and early 2003 and then taking over Education Science and Training until the 2004 election.

Harmer did his doctorate at the University of NSW in Urban Economics and Urban Geography and came into the public service because of his research background. "I delivered a paper on residential renewal in Sydney and in the audience was a senior public servant from that department," he says. "He asked me was I interested in coming to Canberra to work on this particular topic and given that the salary he was offering was at least a couple of times higher than I was being paid as a University tutor I decided that was a good move."

Originally it was on an 18 month contract. "I enjoyed the research area but ... I really enjoyed being able to make a difference in policy so I moved quickly into the policy area. I've been in policy, practically ever since ... I enjoyed the idea that you could make a difference in what I regard as the most important business in the country. Talking motivationally to my staff about the importance of working in government I talk about having the Green and Gold jersey on when you're working for the Australian Government."

Harmer says that over the years there have been a lot of things that he would have liked to have done differently. He does not recall any major blunders, however. "Perhaps that's why I've managed to get through the system and get to the top," he says. The little things he recalls going wrong are occasions when "you've written a brief for the minister and you discover the figures used were out of date and the minister has referred to them in Parliament. Or you've briefed the minister for a meeting with a key stakeholder and no one bothered to check what the key issue for the discussion was going to be. You interpreted what you thought they were going to talk to the minister about and you got it wrong."

He says that when one finds a mistake such as wrong figures, it is essential to own up immediately. "Try and update it and explain it to the minister. Usually you get a kick in the butt for getting it wrong. But you have to accept that. Not everyone gets it right all of the time. But you have to be professional. You can't hide things. One of the things I've learnt in my public service career is that when you do discover something's gone wrong, or you've given the wrong information, or whatever, you have to very, very quickly correct it, whether it be at Senate Estimates, a brief to the minister or whatever. There is absolutely no doubt that you'll get yourself into more trouble trying to hide things, than you do making them transparent. But everyone makes mistakes. I also have a philosophy that it's best not to be too heavy in your criticism of staff for their first mistake. You should say, 'what have you learnt?' and 'what would you put in place to make sure it doesn't happen again?'"

Harmer says staff do learn from mistakes. But if staff are made too risk averse, "You won't get the creativity you need". "So I'm very careful about not punishing people too much and I think my ministers understand that too. Harmer is proud of his work on key policy initiatives over the years such as remodelling the housing assistance programs, the first home owners' scheme, transformational change in the Health Insurance Commission and re-negotiating a number of Commonwealth-State Agreements in housing, supported accommodation, mental health and disability programs.

Harmer has done quite a bit of Commonwealth-State negotiation and says among other things it requires a very good knowledge of the subject matter. "You can get yourself into difficulty very quickly in multilateral negotiations with state officials because they tend to stay in their areas of expertise and not move around quite as much as we do in the Commonwealth," he said. "And they're very experienced at getting money out of the Commonwealth and trying to do as little as they possibly can for it. Commonwealth negotiators have to be very careful when dealing with the states on joint programs. I've usually managed to develop good relationships with my state counterparts which has helped. We often have debates and disagreements. But if you can call them and talk about it off line from time to time, that helps a lot. I think building good relations, whether it be within the Commonwealth across departments or between the Commonwealth and the states is absolutely critical to be an effective senior public servant. I don't know how anyone can really expect to be an effective leader and effective in serving a minister unless they're good at managing external and internal relations."

Harmer is an early starter, who does some exercise every morning before coming into work between 7.30 and 7.45. "I close my door until 9 o'clock and that hour and a half, hour and a quarter I get a lot of my reading done, planning for the day, thinking about strategy, reading the press clippings and that sort of thing. I open my door at 9 o'clock and then my day is typically a series of meetings with one or other of my senior colleagues. One or two meetings with external people, either a stakeholder group, or someone from another department. I, of course, have regular meetings with the minister."

Frequently he represents the department at meetings ranging from indigenous issues to portfolio secretaries' meetings and senior level inter departmental committees. He also actively contributes to the broader public service by speaking at Public Service Commission courses for senior executives and on leadership to groups of executives. In a typical week he usually spends up to a day outside Canberra – visiting state offices or attending meetings with key stakeholders. When Senate Estimates are on there is not only the attendance but also the practice sessions with group managers beforehand. He finishes his day at 6 o'clock or a little later.

"I have a firm view that I won't be very effective the next day unless I get a reasonable amount of relaxation. I constantly say to my staff that I'm impressed by what they do while they're here, rather than how long they're here. I'm interested in outcomes and outputs, rather than inputs. I don't judge people by how long they're at work. That is an input. I've been in places where that has been the case but I certainly don't believe in that approach. When people have completed their work for the day I want to see them going home to their families. I think staff productivity will be higher if they have high morale and I strongly believe that high morale comes from good leadership, (and I put a lot of effort into that with my senior executives)."

Harmer points to the leadership behaviours he has recently established as part of the FaCS strategic framework. They are to set the direction, provide clear and consistent guidance to staff, achieve results, set the example and value and develop staff. "I constantly remind my senior managers of their responsibilities in these areas and constantly put pressure on managers to improve their leadership. This is the most certain way I know to improve morale and therefore productivity. There are some who believe that the best way to high productivity is through financial incentives but I don't believe this is what motivates public servants."

Harmer says he regards it as a very important part of his job to maintain good relations with his colleague secretaries and agency heads. "It doesn't mean agreeing with them all the time," he says. "Sometimes we have fundamental disagreements, including in our regular meetings. That's quite healthy. But never to the point where it becomes a personal issue. I never play the man (or woman), it's always the ball."

This article was first published in the Canberra Times on 19 December 2005

The Unabashed Rationalist – Peter Boxall, Department of Employment and Workplace Relations

The Secretary of the Department of Employment and Workplace Relations, Peter Boxall, came very close to leaving Australia and settling in the United States. After living in America for 13 years, where he worked for the International Monetary Fund and completed a doctorate at the University of Chicago, Boxall returned to Australia in 1986. "It took me a while to settle back into Australia," he says. "I was single at the time. I found it fairly difficult because I'd lived for so long outside and I nearly didn't make it. I nearly left and went back to the US."

Boxall says there were cultural differences and he didn't have any family in Australia. His parents had both passed away and his one brother had left Australia in 1973. Boxall was brought up on a small farm at Scotts Creek, near Timboon and Port Campbell in Southern Victoria. His parents settled on a block surrounded by bush, including crown land, in 1948. A previous occupant had cleared about an acre of land and built a two room shack with lean-to verandas. It was fairly tough going, raising pigs for a living and milking a few cows on the side. "We always ate well and we were well dressed. But that was about the extent of it," he says.

Boxall went to school at Timboon consolidated, an experiment by the Victorian Education department to set up an alternative to the one teacher and two teacher schools in country areas. Class sizes were reasonable because the school drew from the farming and local area and Boxall estimates he was in a class of about 25. Of these, three or four later made it to University.

Boxall went to Ballarat Grammar Boarding school in year nine. "It was a huge sacrifice ... but my parents valued education. I came from a very supportive family, a very loving family. When I first went to boarding school I was terribly homesick. My mother knew the value of education having gone to a private school herself in Melbourne and finished matriculation, which was quite something for a woman in those days. I grew up in an area where you're encouraged to be independent because you're living on a farm. There are lots of jobs to do. I really loved it. I plan, when I finish these CEO type jobs ... to buy a dairy farm. I have a young family so when my youngest daughter finishes year 12, I plan to hang up the shingle."

After graduating in 1971, Boxall joined the Reserve Bank where he stayed for three years. He then moved to the United States. Arriving back in Australia in 1986, in his late thirties and having lived more than a third of his life in the US,

Boxall had the option of going to Treasury or the private financial sector in Sydney. "For some reason I gravitated to Treasury where the pay in those days was quite low – very low after tax ... I was interested in public policy work with my economics background and my general interests."

He was also drawn to Canberra because he would have easy access to the bush and rural pursuits. In Chicago Boxall came into contact with leading economists. Two of his PhD supervisors, Gary Becker and Robert Lucas, have since won Nobel Prizes. The third, the late labour economist, Sherwin Rosen, was president of the American Economics Association.

The University's economics faculty gained fame – some would say notoriety – from the active campaigning in the 1970s of monetarist economist Milton Friedman. Boxall says Friedman had retired by the time he went to the University but he did go to a lecture Friedman gave. "It was great. He just got up and he said, 'I won't give a lecture. I'll answer questions'. There were about 10 or 11 questions. All but one I thought were good questions. It was really great. I enjoyed the University of Chicago so much. It was an incredibly stimulating environment. The quality of the faculty was first rate."

Boxall has the reputation of believing in the 'rational economic man'. The question he says is: "how does the person at the margin operate?" "If you have an incentive structure, if you increase or decrease a price, then you will elicit a response from an individual or a firm at the margin. I believe that happens. I think it's very clear that happens. I think the data, the analysis and the evidence is unarguable." The reaction does not have to be from everyone. "There might be a bunch of people who might keep on doing things more or less indefinitely irrespective of what happens to the price. But the fact is that if you increase the price more people are likely to supply and less people are likely to demand it." The other issue he says which is related, but which is not quite the same point, is the impact on business. "The fact is people in the business sector have a bottom line and if you impose too many costs on them, they go out of business."

Boxall has a young family, one daughter aged seven and another aged eleven. He says this is one reason why he will have to work for ten more years in the sort of job he is in. Unlike many other department heads Boxall does not work twelve hour days. "I get to work normally about 9 o'clock and I normally leave about six," he says. "I try not to work on weekends. And I try not to work in the evenings, apart from official functions and apart from meetings that are called at 8.30 am. Every now and then I have to do a little bit of email at night or on Sunday night just to clear the decks and make sure it hasn't backed up on me."

His wife Karen Chester works three days a week in an intensive job as CEO of Access Economics, and he says work/family balance is a big issue for him. In line with this he says he tries to be considerate of his staff. "We don't normally call meetings before 9.30 in the morning and we try not to call meetings after about 4.30 in the afternoon. This is so people can come to work, not be rushed."

Boxall applies a trusting, or some might say risky, process to handling ministerial briefs. Unlike many senior managers who clear briefs before they leave the department, Boxall's system allows his executives to send briefs direct to the minister's office without his prior approval. The executives are expected to discuss the issues with Boxall first, and then prepare the brief and send it to the minister. "I read the brief electronically," he says. "I read the summary and then, if I need to, I read the whole brief. If I find there is something in there that is not quite right, I pull the brief and we re-do it." By that stage the brief may have gone to the minister but Boxall says he usually gets to it before the minister has had a chance to read it.

This process, he says, avoids a bottleneck. "If I had to clear everything in what is one of the biggest departments in Canberra and certainly has been the busiest in the last 12 months – we've had Welfare to Work and Work Choices plus the tender round for the Job Network – it would just be unmanageable." But what if he is too busy and does not get to the brief? "I'm now in my tenth year as a secretary at the Commonwealth level, five years in Finance and in my fifth year here and only once has a minister got to something that I wanted to pull, before I pulled it."

On average he pulls a brief about once a month. Lately this might have risen to 1.5 a month because of increased volume of business. Boxall says managers accept that briefs get pulled. "They're fine about it. They know how it works … I send them an email or I call them up and they pull it immediately. And then we just rejig it or we might rewrite it. Usually it's rejigged."

Boxall says he really likes his job as head of DEWR. "I had a background in labour economics, had an interest in it and I find the job intellectually stimulating." Boxall has a reputation of being one of the 'economic rationalists' in the public service. "I'm proud of it," he says when this is put to him. "I like to think of myself as a classic liberal. I think that the market has so much to offer and that there are a few areas where the Government might intervene, for political reasons, or for other reasons, usually to do with redistribution of income and issues like that. But I think the Australian based market economy has done very well, as have the other market economies."

Boxall thinks his upbringing on a small farm in Victoria has influenced his thinking. There he witnessed tough times but he also sees it an issue of independence, an issue of being able to do things for yourself rather than having to wait for others to help. "Of course some people need help if they're in a tight spot," he says. "But usually there's an issue between receiving help when you're in a tight spot and help on an on-going basis. There's an issue of people's personal pride, self esteem, being able to do things for themselves, being able to make choices, being able to send their kids to the school that they want to."

He says he respects the political process which determines the point of intervention. "The people vote for the Government and then the Government needs to make a judgement about where it's going to intervene, to what extent it's going to redistribute, to what extent it's going to assist certain groups in the community. And that's the result of the political process and that's a call for the elected representatives. Our job as public servants is to advise on the public policy aspects, to point out the pros and cons of certain alternative policies and to be able to analyse them so that ministers have a full information set when they act – in particular to point out unintended consequences, both positive and negative. This is an issue which goes to equity and fairness. Equity and fairness is a value judgement. It's not something that economists or engineers or anybody else has a particular expertise in. Something that I think is fair, you might think is unfair. That's why it has to be a decision taken by politicians who are the elected representatives who have contact with their electorates."

"It's really our job to look at what is efficient, which is more measurable, and effective and ethical. And that's why in the FMA Act [Financial Management and Accountability Act under which Commonwealth departments operate] they have this section ... which says that one of the duties of CEOs such as myself is the three Es: efficient, effective and ethical use of taxpayers money. Fairness is an issue for the politicians."

Boxall is one of the small number of department heads, which includes Michael L'Estrange at Foreign Affairs and Trade, who have worked as an advisor in the politicians' offices. Having spent years in the public sector he took a job with Deputy Opposition Leader, Andrew Peacock, and helped prepare the opposition's 1990 economic action plan. Later, when the Coalition was elected to Government he was Chief of Staff in Treasurer, Peter Costello's office.

Few doubt the difficulties Oppositions face in trying to draw up a comprehensive and defensible economic plan with the limited staff and financial resources available. Mistakes are costly and the best staff are required. Boxall says by the time he was employed by Peacock he was well aware of the issues confronting the Opposition and was relatively experienced having worked at the Reserve Bank and the International Monetary Fund where, with colleagues, he had prepared macro economic plans. "You're at a disadvantage in a sense, but that's Opposition," he says.

Boxall's department has taken on additional responsibilities and grown to over 3000 staff in the five years he has been there. "As I see it my job is to be what they now call a producer manager," he says. "Not only do you have to run the department so that you produce the outputs, which are advice to Government, often in the form of ministerial briefs, but we also deliver a number of services on behalf of government such as the Employee Entitlements Scheme. We have a number of other service delivery aspects to our work so we provide what we claim to be high quality advice and also deliver services on behalf of the Government. My job is to keep on delivering those services and the way I do that is primarily through the selection of very good staff. I have a very good SES [Senior Executive Service]."

"I was lucky when I came to the department to inherit a good team of SES and I've tried to add to that. It's also to devise a compensation scheme which encourages people to give of their best. But on top of that I need to keep my finger on the pulse, on the policy advice that's going to a minister. I need to intervene when I see something that's not quite going on track." And the same with the service delivery. "So it's very much a role of being in touch with my SES, being able to access all the ministerial briefs through the electronic network, being on top of issues of service delivery and being ready to intervene. The way I've operated, I've devolved the responsibility to my managers, who in turn devolve it to their managers and it cascades right down through the department."

Boxall says his department has clear objectives because he and his executive have given a lot of thought to them. They aim for three outcomes – employment, workplace relations and workplace participation. He says the ministers of the elected government are their "customers". "We serve job seekers and other clients of the department on behalf of ministers. It's very clear where the accountability is."

As head of Finance, Boxall was responsible for the introduction of the system of accruals, outcomes and outputs that is now in place in the service. He says departments have had varying degrees of success in implementing accrual accounting. But what it has done is to get departments to focus on the true cost of service delivery, forcing them to take account of such things as depreciation. The outcomes and outputs were a major improvement because they focused on what the program actually achieved. Where ministers and departments had taken performance indicators seriously, they had been quite successful. "It's not perfect but in my view it's much better than what was there in the past," he says.

But if the unemployment rate went up would he see that as his department's responsibility? "Well, one of the indicators is the state of the labour market and obviously there's more than us that contribute to that," he says. "There's macro economic policy in Treasury, and the Reserve Bank and others."

He says they have a one to one correspondence between each of his three deputies and the three outcomes the department seeks to meet. On the unemployment question he says it is very difficult to disentangle to what extent his department's efforts might be at fault vis à vis other departments. "We just have to try and do our best. The fact is that in my view this is a much better system than we used to have. I think that this is a very important reform, a core budget reform with the outputs and outcomes and it has got the whole public service and for that matter Parliament, focused more on the outcomes and outputs and what we're trying to achieve."

About three quarters of Boxall's department are on an Australian Workplace Agreement and they are eligible for a performance bonus. Boxall says if the unemployment rate went up and it was fairly clear that this was not due to a mismanagement of the employment programs, that would be taken into account in any assessment. But if there was a major mismanagement of the employment programs by senior people in the department they would struggle to get a bonus, whether the unemployment rate went up or down.

The immediate challenges for the department are the implementation of Work Choices and the Welfare to Work agenda. The department must also continue reform of the Community Development Employment Program and increase indigenous employment. Finally there is the successful tendering of the Job Network and other services.

On indigenous employment Boxall says he thinks gradually something is happening and things are moving in the right direction. Passage of the Work Choices legislation and associated regulations will result in his department having a bigger role in the compliance arrangements. In Treasurer Peter Costello's office, Boxall worked on the Coalition Government's first Budget where major expenditure cuts were introduced. He says he has been through six Expenditure Review Committees, possibly as many as anybody in Canberra, apart from the Treasurer.

Asked if in cutting the first deficit there was anything that caused him anguish, he says, "No. I don't recall actually. It was quite interesting that the public service didn't seem well prepared for it and a lot of it was driven by the new ministers." In doing this he says they met resistance, including from central agencies. He agrees that he has wielded the knife for a fair bit of his career and, when asked if he prefers this to doling out money he says, "I would not prefer to be doling out money because I have great respect for taxpayers' money and I don't like supporting programs which I don't think are good value for the taxpayer." But if he was given a social security type portfolio he says he would happily administer it "because I'm a professional public servant and if the Government decides that they should pay money to certain groups of people then I will pay it. But as a policy adviser it doesn't mean to say I would recommend that they do that."

He considers himself a classic liberal and thinks there is scope to continue to look at government expenditure in a lot of areas to see whether programs are really necessary. This applies even when there is a significant surplus because then there can be lower taxes. Boxall says when he was secretary of Finance from 1997 to 2002 he was subjected to quite a focussed hostile campaign. While his stance had the backing of the Government he believes he and some other secretaries were attacked as a way of attacking the Government. He will not say who precisely instigated the attacks. "Did it make my life uncomfortable? Not terribly. It wasn't very pleasant."

When asked if he was more closely aligned with the views of Max Moore-Wilton, he replied "Look, I don't really know because Max Moore-Wilton was head of PM&C and it's difficult when people are head of PM&C to work out what their real views are. That's not a criticism of him ... because you've got to be a collegiate player ... because I was secretary of Finance I didn't have to be a collegiate player to the same extent."

Today, do more secretaries share his views or does he think he is at one end of the spectrum? "I think there are a spectrum of views of other secretaries. Not all other secretaries share my philosophical approach. Not all other secretaries have the same background as me. And so in many respects I am different."

This article was first published in the Canberra Times on 27 March 2006

Environmental Angler – David Borthwick, Department of Environment and Heritage

It was late at night in the old Parliament House when Treasury official David Borthwick plucked up the courage to intervene in the Expenditure Review Committee deliberations chaired by Prime Minister, Bob Hawke. "I could see that they were going to make what I thought was a wrong decision based on incorrect information," he says. So I decided to speak up just before they took the decision, to explain that there were some factors that they didn't know about. As I was making the explanation, I saw Paul Keating [the Treasurer] gripping the edge of the table and his knuckles going very white. At that stage I started breaking out in perspiration and not looking at him. Anyway, about 15 minutes later, after I'd made this explanation he said 'I want to see you outside'."

In the old Parliament House, Borthwick recalls, they had old cast iron water heaters. "Keating got me in the corridor and my back was against the wall, pressed against this water heater and he stood about 18 inches from me and let fly. He knew what was being decided was wrong. But he was setting a trap to spring on his colleagues and I'd prematurely sprung it." Borthwick says it was "colourful, colourful Keatingesque style language." During the exchange, Defence, Science and Personnel minister, Ros Kelly walked down the corridor, saw what was happening and immediately turned around and went the other way.

Borthwick came back to Treasury to report to his then Deputy Secretary, Chris Higgins, and Division Head, David Morgan. "I walked into Morgan's office and said, 'my career's ruined. The Treasurer's lost confidence in me. I'll have to go to another position. I can't front up tomorrow because he won't put trust in me.' They just burst out laughing and said, 'you've just got to get back in the saddle and go on with it'. And I did." Borthwick says what followed were many successful years working with Keating. At his very next meeting with Keating it was as if nothing had happened. "He was like that. He'd said what he needed to say. I'd learnt the lesson."

David Borthwick graduated from Monash University with first class honours in economics and joined the Treasury department in 1973. The son of a former Liberal Deputy Premier of Victoria and possibly the first Environment/Conservation minister in Australia, Bill Borthwick, David has gone on to head the federal Department of the Environment and Heritage. His father died in 2001, never seeing his son in the position.

David's university years were in Monash's radical era. "I was there with Albert Langer, the Vietnam War period and I guess you'd say the riots and protests on campus. I don't know if it's a badge of honour but while the other students were protesting I was sitting in the Library swatting. That's probably why I did pretty well."

While Monash may have been radical overall, its Economics Faculty with such people as Richard Snape, Fred Gruen and Di Yerbury followed conventional lines. When Borthwick moved to Canberra in 1973, Treasury was headed by Sir Frederick Wheeler. "It was an exciting time because the Labor Government had come into power and basically I guess they lost the plot. [There was] a huge burst in APS wages, a huge burst in outlays to GDP because they were impatient to make change."

Borthwick left Treasury in 1974, joining the Industries Assistance Commission under the hugely influential Alf Rattigan, the father of economic rationalism in Australia. In 1979 he came back to Treasury as a branch head. Bernie Fraser, who went on to become Secretary of Treasury and Governor of the Reserve Bank, was his first division head. Borthwick was 28. He says he was lucky that he had a whole sequence of senior Treasury people like the late Chris Higgins, who became Secretary, David Morgan, who now heads the Westpac Bank and Bernie Fraser who actively assisted him in his career and growth.

In Treasury for 19 years from 1979 to 1998, he headed three branches, including the Overseas Finance Branch that looked after the balance of payments and the exchange, at the time of floating of the dollar in 1983. At the time the Secretary of Treasury, John Stone, opposed the float but Borthwick says he supported the float. "It's come out subsequently that there was quite an internal debate which Treasury was famous for," he says. "It's not a monolithic organisation. There were different views in Treasury at the time. But I was right in the thick of that."

After the floating of the dollar in 1983, Paul Keating made his famous Banana Republic comment and there was a major exercise in cutting back outlays. In 1985-86 outlays were 27.3 per cent of GDP. Borthwick proudly points to the fact that over the following years, when he was the relevant branch head and later division head in charge of fiscal policy, outlays as a percentage of GDP were reduced by 4.9 percentage points – equivalent in today's dollars to about $36 billion. "That reduction in outlays has never been seen before or since," he says. The cuts came from more targeting of welfare expenditure and Borthwick says it could almost be seen as the start of the Welfare to Work agenda that's running now.

Borthwick then headed Treasury's Structural Policy and Economic Divisions. He was posted as Australian Ambassador to the OECD from 1991 to 1993 but then came back to Treasury to head the Taxation Policy Division before being promoted to Deputy Secretary where he stayed until 1998. He then transferred to the Department of Health as a Deputy Secretary. "The advice to me, and it was wise advice, was that if I aspired to be secretary of a department I could not have a career trajectory which was solely Treasury," he said. The head of the Department of the Prime Minister and Cabinet, Max Moore-Wilton, then brought Borthwick over to his department to do what seems to be the obligatory stint in PM&C for anyone hoping to be a department head. The relationships Borthwick developed as he rose through the service have paid off in his current position.

Joanna Hewitt, the current head of the Department of Agriculture, Fisheries and Forestry was at the OECD at the same time as he was, helping cement the co-operative approach the two departments have developed. "We've got a very close relationship," Borthwick says, "but it was really Roger Beale [former Environment department head] and Mike Taylor [former DAFF head] who forged the relationship between our two departments, which we continue."

Borthwick says he operates as a portfolio secretary, taking broad responsibilities for the portfolio, not just his own agency. Every Monday he meets not just with his department deputies and division heads, but with the heads of the agencies such as the Bureau of Meteorology, the Great Barrier Reef Marine Park Authority and the Director of National Parks who runs parks at Kakadu, Uluru, Booderee, Norfolk Island and Christmas Island.

The location of the parks in the portfolio provides an opportunity to do something positive in one of the problem areas in the public service, indigenous employment. Borthwick says in Uluru, Kakadu in the Northern Territory and Booderee on the South Coast at Jervis Bay, the parks are jointly managed with indigenous Australians. At Booderee, he says, major park services are contracted out to an indigenous corporation with about 35 people from the Wreck Bay community, maintaining the roads and walking trails and cleaning and maintaining the camping grounds. "We've helped the indigenous people establish a business to service the park with opportunities for servicing the council and local community," he says. He adds that all the parks have a large number of indigenous staff. "Our challenge is to get them into senior positions," he says. "We've just appointed our first indigenous park manager at Uluru. This is important because their desire to remain on their country and care for that country, matches what the Park's about."

State parks do not have the same long history of joint management with indigenous people, marking a substantial difference in the way the Commonwealth and the states work (although other jurisdictions are moving towards joint management in some form). Borthwick says each Monday his portfolio managers' meeting provides a snapshot of what's on. "I try and not lose myself in detail. I try to focus on the major strategic positioning of the department – what elements of our business can we do better, or refine?"

He says he is in daily contact with ministerial staff and the minister is readily available. "His view is if I need to speak to him, just get on the phone. If you don't help the Government of the day manage the day to day issues, get on the front foot, snuff out inaccuracies or anticipate issues, governments and ministers soon lose confidence in you," he says. "Then you can't achieve the big things. So inevitably a lot of Secretaries' time – it's not unique to me – is spent on day-to-day issues."

Borthwick differs from all other secretaries interviewed on the issue of over-scrutiny of the service. "That's a view probably I don't share, to tell the truth," he says. "If I'm a CEO of a private corporation, I'm subject to daily scrutiny through the stock market, up and down daily scrutiny ... for the public sector it's very important, when you haven't got that market discipline, to find other ways to make sure there's scrutiny and that extends right from the accountability of ministers to the Parliament, the executive government to the Parliament and for us through the various parliamentary committees, or the ombudsman or the ANAO (the Australian National Audit Office). So my own view is that it's completely appropriate that we run transparent and open systems. And that's not restricted to policy matters either. We have been, and will remain, completely open with our staff exposed to contamination of their drinking water. I will make sure that they know everything we know about the risks they face. That they know – and expect – us to be transparent, is one of the reasons they have responded so well to this disturbing development."

The irony of the Environment department being a victim of an environmental problem is not lost on Borthwick who vows he will do everything possible to see it explained and rectified. "[I]f we're before an estimates committee, we can be asked searching questions and sometimes it becomes personalised in terms of thinking that the public servants are running a political agenda. We're not. We're to run the agenda of the Government of the day. It's very clear. I just think it's part of the system and it's not going to go away."

A stuffed trout, surrounded by photos of prize trout catches, features in a corner of Borthwick's office in the John Gorton Building in Parkes. Proudly he points out that he caught the fish in the Googong dam and that one of the photos shows a 28½ inch (72.4 centimetres) brown trout he hooked in Spencer Creek. "I thought long and hard about whether I should put those photos, and the fish, on the wall," Borthwick says. "And I wanted to make it clear to people that things like our parks, and our outdoors, are there to enjoy for everybody. I wasn't going to shy away from what I like doing. It's a bit of a statement." Borthwick is well aware that trout are feral but quips, "I reckon they've been here for about 150 years and they've been naturalised."

These are not the sorts of comments that would endear the Environment department secretary to the environmental purists but Borthwick does not seem too concerned. He sees his function as delivering the Government's environment policies. Borthwick points out that the focus on the environment is a relatively new thing. In earlier years, he says, the focus was always on exploiting forests, exploiting water, getting the most out of the land. "Over the last 30 years the balance has tipped. I see my challenge as getting the balance right, between pursuing environmental objectives, and the Government and the people's aspirations to pursue economic and social objectives."

Twenty years or so ago, he says, the department acted more like an environmental group, staking a position in the sand and taking no prisoners. "Well that was ineffective for a Government department. So what we've tried to do is operate to clear environmental objectives but try and balance them with broader economic and social objectives. I see that as the main change – pre-dating me – in the way that the department has evolved over time."

Part of this change is the more co-operative way the department works with other departments such as the Agriculture, Fisheries and Forestry (DAFF) and Industry, Tourism and Resources (DITR). DAFF and the Environment department run a joint, four branch division, looking after land and water management. Under an agreement signed with the Secretary of DAFF, Joanna Hewitt, common briefing notes go to the Environment and the Agriculture, Forestry and Fisheries ministers. "In other words, we're not like warring cousins," Borthwick says. "We're delivering a common objective." Where there are differences, "We work them out in the main but where we don't work them out, we highlight the differences to ministers. [It's] the public service acting as it should. It's whole of government working in practice." He agrees with Hewitt's comments in an earlier interview that this is dramatically different to how things operated twenty years ago. In part this relationship is helped by the fact that the two secretaries worked together as economists at the Australian mission to the OECD in the early 1990s.

Borthwick says the public service he joined in 1973 in the Treasury was a service where secretaries of departments spent more time arguing with one another and carving out fiefdoms than trying to reform the Australian economy, or put the social system in good straits. As the economy was deregulated, the exchange rate floated and protection cut across the board, the senior echelons of the public service changed. People who were interested in making a difference, and improving the lot of the Australian people overall triumphed over people who identified their department's interests as protecting their stakeholders. Part of this change was due to the rise of managerialism, or increasing professionalism. "In the public sector I joined, graduates were in a minority. Overwhelmingly they're [now] in a majority."

Borthwick says the Australian Constitution does not really define the role for the Commonwealth in the environment area. "What the current government did when it came into power was to say, "Well, let's stop this argument of Commonwealth versus state. Let's try and define what is the Commonwealth's role in the environment and what is the state's role in the environment." The end result was a detailed memorandum of understanding, agreed by the Council of Australian Governments (COAG), setting out the division of responsibility. The then Environment minister, Senator Robert Hill, translated this into the Environment Protection and Biodiversity Conservation Act (EPBC Act).

Today he says they have mechanisms by which the views of different stakeholders can be raised. There is an independent Threatened Species Scientific Committee advising on what flora or fauna should be listed. These lead to recovery plans, which then affect development approvals. There is also the Australian Heritage Council advising on what should be on the National Heritage list. Borthwick says the EPBC Act decisions are subject to frequent appeals through the court system making it "a very transparent open process".

Borthwick does not believe his economics training puts him out of place in the environment department. "I don't think it's a disadvantage," he says. Historically governments tackled environmental issues through regulatory action such as 'thou shalt not clear land' directives. But there is a clear place for market instruments. For example, the introduction of the national water initiative a few years ago opened up the water markets to trading and separated the water title from the land title. "Water can trade from low value uses in agriculture, for example, to higher value uses," he says. "At the same time you can enter the water market, and if government so decides, purchase water back for the environment. There's lots of avenues for bringing market instruments to bear." Similarly he says the Government's recent decision to buy out fishing licences in the South Eastern part of Australia will make use of market instruments to put the fisheries in that area on a sustainable basis – a coincidence of achieving environmental objectives partly through economic measures and partly through regulatory measures.

Asked if environmentalists were critical of the economist's approach he says there are such critics but adds that he wasn't the one who led this change. "We weren't in the game in the past," he says. "It's no use feeling fantastic if no-one's listening to you. You've got to be in the game. If you talk the same language, do the rigorous analysis, engage with the industry departments, engage with the community and get the balance right, you'll achieve your objectives."

As in other departments, Borthwick says, they do not have a monolithic view. "We've got people who would be, and are a lot happier, taking a pretty pure view. And it's important that we do have a range of perspectives in the department." He says that the department needs scientists to identify environmental problems and they need them to work with other professional groups. Once a problem is identified, the department must work out the best mix of measures to tackle it. The changes should not be made "in a sudden burst of activity". "The degradation of the environment took a long time. It took generations … you know the old soldier settlers who cleared the land weren't motivated by environmental vandalism. Their state of knowledge wasn't good enough at that stage. As knowledge improves, we've got to find pathways to fix things up. But in the main it will take a long time to repair river ways, land use patterns. The trick is to work with farmers, to work with business, and not so much work against them, and to treat them fairly in the adjustment. Then you'll start making a difference. But if you just say, 'No, this is the Soviet style approach – thou shalt not do it' – it'll be counter productive and it'll rebound on us. So I think we're in the game … but there'll always be arguments about, 'have we struck the balance right?' And that'll change over time."

The major challenges Borthwick sees for the department are: administering the National Heritage Trust with DAFF; giving effect to the Government policy on regional marine planning and marine parks; the national water initiative; and solving the greenhouse problem. The $3 billion National Heritage Trust program requires working with the states and local communities across 56 catchments. Borthwick says they aim to get some solid measurable results on the ground and there are exciting possibilities "but it will take time". The Government put out a draft plan for eleven new marine parks off Victoria and Tasmania before Christmas. The parks are two and a half times the size of Tasmania and Borthwick sees the challenge as integrating them with the fishing, petroleum and mining industries' aspirations. "The third major challenge is to make the Government's historic national water initiative work effectively," he says. "It's a ten year plan in terms of what has to be done and when. It will both increase agricultural productivity and benefit the environment."

He says Australia is in a unique position in facing the global greenhouse problem because the Government has decided not to ratify Kyoto, but to meet the Kyoto target. Australia chairs the umbrella group which has America, Russia, Japan, New Zealand, Canada, Norway, Ukraine, Iceland and other countries. "We're in a very influential position," he says. He says the fact that Australia is one of the biggest per capita greenhouse gas emitters reflects the distances Australians travel because the small population lives in a big country. It also reflects our strong resource based economy: mining coal unlocks greenhouse emissions.

Because of Australia's unique features the country's Kyoto target was set at 108 per cent of 1990 emissions. Australia's coal exports success means more greenhouse gases are being unlocked. But, Borthwick says, the world is highly dependent on fossil fuel and all the projections from the International Energy Agency and other bodies say that for the next 50 years the world will be 80 per cent dependent on them. "That's the reality. Nuclear won't take it over. Renewables won't take it over. Natural gas won't take it over. The world's going to be dependent on coal for a long time. We're a rich source of coal. So a lot of Australia's effort will go into trying to clean up those coal technologies. It's in our interests because that's the way the world will be. Electricity generating facilities have an economic life of 30, 40 50 years. It's going to be burnt. So the effort needs to be in cleaning it up."

This article was first published in the Canberra Times on 9 January 2006

Keeping the Customer Satisfied – Robert Cornall, Attorney-General's Department

In February 2000, shortly after his appointment as head of the Attorney-General's Department, Robert Cornall delivered a speech to his senior executive service telling them of his initial thoughts about the department. In his address Cornall, who was an outside appointment, said that when he was interviewed for the position and asked his views about the Attorney-General's, he replied that it was a prestigious department, held in high regard and it would be an honour to be appointed Secretary. After a month in the job he said his initial expectation had been confirmed. He was impressed by the overall calibre and experience of the staff. But he added there were "some important issues to be resolved".

In particular he noted two findings highlighted by research into the department's performance. He noted that senior management placed a significantly higher priority on quality of service than on client satisfaction. While the emphasis on quality of service was commendable, client service could be improved. The other finding that caught his eye was that the department's employees placed "inwardly focusing factors" in the top ten most important rankings. "[T]here is a very clear message that the department needs to develop its outward or client focus to improve its performance," he said.

To drive home the point, Cornall quoted one department secretary saying that the Attorney-General's Department was "not a player" and another senior bureaucrat saying that the Government was "looking for someone to ground" the department. These perceptions indicated dissatisfaction with the department's level of performance. But Cornall said he understood them to be more "disappointed than critical".

Today after six years in the job Cornall speaks proudly of his department's achievements, its increased areas of responsibility, the diversity of its activities, the 145 Acts of Parliament it administers, the contribution its Emergency Management Australia Division made in Australia's response to the Boxing Day tsunami, its increasing participation with other departments, its adaptability and its international role. He says he put his speech outlining his initial impressions on the web and invited all staff to comment. "A lot of people did. And that was the basis of moving forward from there."

His view that client satisfaction should be given greater emphasis was influenced by his years as a private sector solicitor. "If you're a private sector solicitor you're always working in a team of at least two people. There's at least yourself and your client. People don't pay you to just go away and do whatever you feel like doing. You've always got to be working in conjunction with someone, to some common objective. So I've always thought that's what we're doing here. The point I was trying to emphasise is that quality of work by itself is very valuable but it's got to be in the context of achieving someone's objective. It's not just for the purity of the advice. It's got to be very sound advice but it's got to have some purpose to it apart from being intellectually stimulating."

Cornall says the department has changed over his six years and the evidence is in what has happened to it. "First, I hope we are perceived to be a cooperative department working with other agencies across departmental and portfolio boundaries. And I think we are and I think that's the perception people have. Secondly, how has government reacted? And the answer is it has given us more things to do. We've grown from something like 550 full time equivalent staff in the year 2001 – if you put aside a couple of major divisional agencies which were not core department – to about 950 at the end of last year. The reason for that is we've been given more functions. We've increased dramatically our responsibility in the areas of national security and that includes developing the National Security Hotline and building up the Watch Office to a 24 hours a day, seven days a week operation. We've had Emergency Management Australia transferred from the Department of Defence to this department on the basis that it will fit more neatly with our national security responsibilities. We received the indigenous law and justice program when ATSIC was abolished."

"The Attorney announced at the end of last year that we're going to be responsible for the creation of this new central vetting agency for aviation security identification cards and maritime security identification cards, which is a major undertaking. We're leading the development of a national identity security plan for the whole of government. We've got a whole range of other responsibilities in terms of critical infrastructure protection that we have taken on in recent years. And we're developing significant improvements to family law including the establishment of the 65 family relationship centres that have been announced in the course of the last 12 months, the first of which come on stream in the middle of this year. The point I make about that is, we would not have acquired all those additional responsibilities if the Government wasn't confident that we were going to meet those requirements."

Cornall says people do not have a full grasp of the breadth of his department's responsibility. "[I]f you look at the range of topics that we cover from copyright to criminal law, from legislative drafting to national security, from emergency management to issues to do with courts and judicial processes, I don't think many people have an overall grasp of how broad our activities are." Nothing illustrates this diversity better than the inclusion of Emergency Management Australia as a division in what most would regard as the law and justice department. EMA played a major role in Australia's efforts to assist those affected by the Boxing Day tsunami and is a key agency in responding to disasters in Australia. To accommodate this diversity the department's mission statement says the department provides essential expert support to the Government for "Australia's law and justice, and national security, and emergency management systems".

Cornall says the three things that are looming very large for the coming year are the establishment of the security vetting service, the development of the identity security plan and the changes to family law including the family relationship centres. The security vetting service will clear people to hold an aviation or maritime security identification card which will last for two years. Staff will be employed in an operating division of the department to run the service which will require liaison with private sector organisations and state government agencies. These will include port and airport authorities where those requiring the identification card will work. "It's going to require us to develop a data base which includes information relating to criminal convictions that might affect people's entitlement to have a security clearance," Cornall says. The details have yet to be finalised but he says they will have to work out what information is readily available, how they can get it into the database and so on. "At any one time when the whole program is operational there could be as many as 120,000 of these identification cards on issue," he says. "So it's going to be a very significant undertaking. It's going to be very important that we get it right."

The family relationship centres are designed to try to strengthen marriage. Cornall says if a marriage breaks up and there are children involved, separated parents will undertake three-hour consultations to try to find ways in which they might resolve their differences about the children without the necessity to go to court and the time, inconvenience, emotion and cost that that brings. The first 15 of those centres will be operational by the middle of this year. The third major challenge is the development of an overall identity security policy for the Commonwealth, bringing with it the controversy over a national identity card. Cornall says this is "a very big question and it affects a lot of agencies." He says it also includes the development of a document verification service to enable the validation of the documents people use to support their claim that they are who they say they are. In the case of a driver's licence, for example, the verification service would be able to go back to the state or territory authority and get them to confirm that it did issue the licence to the specified person. This will give increased credibility to the integrity of the document and make identity fraud more difficult.

He says he spends a lot of time trying to anticipate what might go wrong and working hard to make sure that problems are headed off. Cornall says if something goes wrong his focus is always on how to fix it and stop it from occurring again. "I don't waste a lot of time on looking for, or attributing blame, or being highly critical of what's occurred. The focus is much more on, okay this is the situation, how can we fix it? The second thing is how can we make sure it doesn't happen again? But if it does occur again, then we've got a more serious problem on our hands."

The heads of Australian Government departments are generally regarded as a serious bunch of individuals. And they have no more serious a gathering than the meeting of the Secretaries Committee on National Security (SCONS). But even SCONS meetings have their lighter moments. Cornall recalls one meeting where they were discussing the Defence Force's Nulka missiles. The Nulka missile is a defensive weapon hovering above warships and giving the impression that it is bigger than the ship, thus providing a decoy against incoming missiles. The former head of the Department of the Prime Minister and Cabinet, Max Moore-Wilton was chairing the meeting but was called out of the room to take a phone call from the Prime Minister. "We were just sitting there waiting for him to come back," Cornall says, "and I said these Nulkas would be pretty handy. I wish we could have one for the department. When Max fired off an Exocet from PM&C it would miss Robert Garran Offices [the home of the Attorney-General's Department] , hit the Nulka missile and explode harmlessly over Kings Avenue and no one would get hurt. And another secretary said, 'Oh we used to have them – they were called ministers'."

In reality Cornall is not the sort of person who would seek to deflect in-coming missiles to his minister. He sees himself very much as a team player. "When I came to Canberra one of the things I had to decide was whether I'd go to Estimates because at that time, I was told, not all Secretaries went. That took me by surprise because I thought, well, it's a matter of accountability to the Parliament. It's a matter of courtesy to the Parliament and it's a matter of being prepared to sit shoulder to shoulder with your senior officers and ensure that as a team you are responding to whatever is being put to you by the Senators. So it never occurred to me not to go."

Cornall began his career in private legal practice as a solicitor in a medium sized firm in Melbourne. He says his 19 years in private practice fixed him in a private sector mindset. "If you didn't have a client who valued your services and was prepared to pay for them, you had nothing to do and you couldn't pay the bills," he says. "We had no expectation that we had a right to exist. We had no expectation that we had a right to clientele. We had to persuade people by various means that they should use services and then we had to convince them that those services were valuable. And I think that's a very useful starting point."

From private practice he moved to become Director of the not-for-profit, member-based, Law Institute of Victoria. The Institute had statutory responsibilities for regulation of the legal profession, taking disciplinary procedures against solicitors for professional misconduct including matters involving misappropriation of trust funds. At the Institute, and with about 135 staff, Cornall was introduced to a whole new range of experiences and procedures. "It underlined to me the merit of proper process because it was quite common for me to be brought before a tribunal, or brought before a court to explain what I had done, or what the organisation had done and for those decisions to be challenged on administrative law or statutory grounds," he says.

At times there were questions about whether the Institute's authority went as far as they thought it did or whether there was some other regulatory structure that should have dealt with the matter. One matter was taken as far as the High Court but the solicitor lost his appeal. Cornall says this sort of experience "does put you on your mettle when your decisions are being reviewed at that level." He says proper process does not have to be "slow or protracted or long winded or cumbersome. You can actually have proper process in a very quick timeframe. But the protection of proper process is very valuable."

After his time at the Institute he became managing director of Victoria Legal Aid, which delivered legal aid services for both the state of Victoria and the Commonwealth within Victoria. In that role he had contact with the Attorney-General's Department and with the then Attorney General, Daryl Williams. "[I]'m not quite sure how it happened but one day Tony Blunn [former head of the Attorney General's Department] rang me up and said that he was proposing to retire and before he retired he wanted to make sure that his successor was in place and would I be interested in talking to him and the Attorney about taking on this job."

"I said that I was and one thing led to another and shortly after that I was appointed by the Prime Minister." Cornall says that on coming to the public sector one of his first the impressions was about how hard the senior public service worked. "Common perceptions about public servants are very, very badly misplaced," he says. "You wouldn't find too many people in the private sector working at 1am on a Sunday morning, if there's some urgent issue requiring attention, or working all weekend to get something up on Monday morning to the Attorney General's office or the Prime Minister. I think the first thing is that people work extremely hard. The second thing is the speed at which decisions are taken. One of the things that struck me is how quickly some significant decisions have been taken."

He says he has witnessed this when he's had the opportunity to sit in on a Cabinet meeting, or the National Security Committee, or the Expenditure Review Committee. "The speed with which decisions are taken, and the volume of decisions in a short period of time, I think is quite impressive," he says. "Decisions on significant matters might be taken in a matter of minutes." This leads him to another observation. "As you get closer to the final decision maker, which might be the Cabinet, or it might be the minister, everything has to be simplified rather than complicated. No matter how complicated the subject matter, the proposal has to be reduced to a very simple proposition."

This has led Cornall to form a view about what he calls the policy pyramid, the idea that at the lowest level, the base of the pyramid there are many research and policy officers developing a proposal, working through the pros and cons and considering all the options. It goes up through the branch head, the division head, deputy secretary and the secretary to the minister. When it actually gets to Cabinet, the minister will have about 20 seconds or 30 seconds to grab people's attention. If in that short period of time he cannot very quickly say what it is about and why it is important, he may lose the moment of getting approval.

Cornall says this emphasises how important the lead-up work is because once the Cabinet or the minister makes the key decision the department has got to be able to completely reconstruct the project to make sure that all the operational parts are properly covered. "You couldn't expect a Cabinet to give that much consideration in detail," he says. "From time to time I've said to the people here, 'tell me in 15 words' because that's how much the minister will have to grab attention in the Cabinet room."

Cornall comes across as a reserved lawyer and says that every time he has lost his temper things have gone badly from that point onwards. "I end up saying things I regret, or making the situation worse, rather than improving it." He says he cannot instantly bring an example to mind but over a period of time he knows that, "if I ever do things rashly, in a fit of temper, it inevitably doesn't get to the best outcome".

He says one of the things he's been very conscious of is the need to be clear in communications and not to use bureaucratic language. "You don't use words that are obtuse, or could have several meanings." Some years back he says the Expenditure Review Committee, chaired by the Treasurer, Peter Costello, was considering a proposal for increasing the number of sniffer dogs. "But that sounded a bit too lightweight. So the submission was for funding for increases for Explosive Detection Canine Capacity. When we were in the Cabinet room the Treasurer said, 'Are these dogs, are they?' And I said, 'Yes Treasurer. They're dogs'. And he said, 'Well what sort of dogs are they?' I looked in my brief and it didn't have any detail. He wanted to know 'how many dogs did we have? Where were the dogs? Who trained them?' So I came back to the department and said in future we've got to have all the obvious basic facts in the briefing paper because they're the sort of things the Treasurer wants to know."

This article was first published in the Canberra Times on 30 January 2006

The Pragmatist – Mike Taylor, Department of Transport and Regional Services

Mike Taylor, head of the Department of Transport and Regional Services believes the great unsung story in Australia at present is the extraordinary road and rail transport policy changes which are currently taking place. "We've started creating a framework where the national AusLink network is now being managed in partnership between the states and the Australian Government, rather than the Australian Government just handing over money, and being unaware of what will, or won't, eventuate," he says.

The AusLink partnership will see some $12 billion spent over the next five years and Taylor believes it will deliver the results the Australian community expects. But he avoids spelling out precisely what these results might be, preferring instead to talk about relationships with the states, and the bi-lateral agreements, including the first signed personally by the Prime Minister.

Taylor has been in the role of Secretary of Transport and Regional Services for 14 months, taking up the position after five years as Secretary of the Department of Agriculture, Forestry and Fisheries. "I'm very much in the business of implementing an important government policy focussed on driving transport reform. Some major initiatives are the way in which we manage road and rail, the aviation and airports policy framework and the maritime framework. Of course the portfolio also has responsibilities in our oversight of territories and regional partnerships," he says.

Taylor observes that the states are the principal builders of roads and have the constitutional power to build them. "All the land acquisition, all the planning controls, all the environment controls, rest with the states," he says. "While the Commonwealth has always been a source of some of the money we have often not been strong in getting the priorities for road expenditure in place. When you look at the freight task in Australia doubling over the next 15 years, you realise that there is a very big challenge out there and Government's must focus on priorities. So an important part of the AusLink policy change is that rather than just the Commonwealth handing over money, it is building strong relationships with the states so that we get a joint approach to future initiatives. It has been important to work from the top down, building a partnership through the Council of Australian Governments' (COAG) framework, producing a commitment to delivering transport reform and infrastructure needs."

A particular part of the COAG transport reform process is the introduction of transport and freight corridor studies, both within and between the states to better understand the future major transport tasks so as to allow priorities to be set more effectively. Taylor points out that the aggregate transport sector represents around 8 per cent of the economy, double agriculture or mining, underlining the significance of the work. He says the big priorities are not necessarily new. In NSW, for example, one is the Hume Highway, the other is addressing the Pacific Highway – the major road corridor between Sydney and Brisbane. This highway has been an issue for a long time.

Quite clearly, Taylor says, we need to lift the level of partnership beyond the traditional transfer of money to NSW with the hope that something develops. So have the Commonwealth and NSW developed a specific agreement on the road? "Well, not yet, however, there are positive developments," he says. "An important issue is that we are moving away from a piecemeal approach, which has been historically slow to deliver results, to one where we get quality and effective road connections all the way between Brisbane and Sydney."

"These are two major economic centres for Australia and we have to make sure the connections work well. To assist this development, we have recently signed a Memorandum of Understanding with the NSW government to explore a wide range of options, including public private partnerships, project management and funding and a broadening of the way in which we might capture the benefits from those who use roads. If we continue the current process it will be extremely slow and the completion of the link to a high level may not happen in our lifetime."

Taylor says his department does not get directly involved in transport policy within the cities as state governments are, have and always will be, dominant for public transport in capital cities. "Under AusLink, part of the way we are working with the states is not just to transfer money into unspecified public transport modes. Instead, the focus is on one of the major issues facing transport in cities; the management of freight movements. So the AusLink framework focuses on how we move freight from ports, both maritime and airport, to inter-modal centres both on road and rail and how we can take that freight out of the mainstream of major cities. This focus is a very important partnership between the two levels of government. That will make a major impact in terms of congestion of freight in cities and that's a big shift in thinking."

Taylor will not hazard a guess as to how long it will be before there is less congestion, preferring to talk about the "Big Picture" and the need to eliminate piecemeal approaches. He agrees a lot of money is required to tackle the issues but says the danger is that everyone talks about the money first. "We've spent a lot of money on the Hume Highway and it's still not completed between Albury and Sydney," he says. "We've spent a lot of money on the Pacific Highway over decades." The big picture is required to get the quantum leaps. "I think the most important shift has been getting the AusLink framework, the partnership between Commonwealth and states, and then the commitment from the Prime Minister and premiers at the COAG meeting last June to the development of the major freight corridor strategies."

On rail, Taylor says the Australian Government is undertaking a major North-South study addressing the movement of freight between Melbourne, Sydney and Brisbane. The Australian Government and the Australian Rail Track Corporation are investing over $2 billion in rail on the AusLink Network primarily to upgrade the vital, north-south rail corridor between Melbourne, Sydney and Brisbane. This investment should improve the competitiveness and efficiency of rail in a corridor where less than 20 per cent is carried by rail, compared with around 80 percent in the east-west corridor. He says the upgrading of railway lines through Sydney and its inner surrounds is complex, "but unless you get your mind around the complexities of the whole corridor, nothing effective will happen in aggregate."

Another major issue Taylor nominates for the department is the territories – Cocos (Keeling) Islands, Christmas Island and Norfolk Island. He says it is very important to work in partnership with these communities. Another major partnership is with local government, where the Government spends more than $1.5 billion a year. Finally, there is the regional partnerships programs contributing to every part of Australia.

Taylor is a committed economic reformer. A former Chief Executive with the Australian Dairy Industry Council and a former head of the Victorian Department of Agriculture, he recalls the restructuring of the Australian dairy industry and the battle by some parties to impose dairy industry quotas. "I was in for freeing up the arrangements," he says. The market was progressively deregulated. The result is that the Australian dairy industry has gone from producing around 5,000 million litres a year in the early 1980s to more than 10,000 million litres a year now. "[I]f it had been restricted by quotas to 5,000 million litres or less there would not only have been reduced employment, there would have been extremely reduced employment opportunities compared to those in the current industry."

Taylor also takes pride in being part of the team that helped drive water policy reforms in Victoria, resulting in the introduction of water property rights for farmers. This, he says, saw water move from low value to high value uses, leading to growth in towns along the Murray River in North West Victoria. The changes also allowed water to be returned to the environment. "[O]ne of the many things I enjoyed, when I came to the Commonwealth, was continuing to work on that process of water reform."

"What's my passion? It's that holistic approach that if you can drive quality economic reform, you can make great improvements in the economy, and consequently the wealth and well being of all Australians, and improve the environment, and improve the social well being of people."

Taylor says his experience in having worked as a head of a state department has not altered the way in which he perceives or deals with the states. "Obviously I operate on the Australian Government's agenda," he says. "I've never seen an awful lot achieved when people hit head on. Invariably, and in the Commonwealth/state framework, whether it's in agriculture, natural resource management, environment, or transport, no one party holds all the cards. So success comes from working effectively with each other."

He says he is a pragmatist who wants to make sure that things happen while he is around. The art of effective public administration is finding a way forward, no matter how bloody minded different parties or individuals might be. "I don't mean you give in on the policy agenda; rather it's about thinking clearly about how I and my team can more effectively communicate what we're seeking to achieve, and underpinning it with quality analysis. It's amazing how when you get good policy analysis , it can begin to make a big difference, provided it is supported by clear and effective communication."

In the water reforms in the late 1980s in Victoria, a team of people in Victoria came up with an effective set of water polices. "However, when we had thousands of farmers marching outside the Parliament, I think the minister of the day understandably thought that while the policy advice may have been very good, the practical implementation had more than a few deficiencies." The policy was dropped at that time, but three or four years later it was successfully re-introduced, by working much more closely with the farming community, the regional community and people with opposing views. "What I'm saying is in the first attempt we got the theory right, however, we hadn't got the implementation or the stakeholders in tune with what we were really trying to do."

Taylor considers himself incredibly fortunate to be in his job. "I think one of the things that's worth saying is that secretaries in the Australian Public Service are very privileged individuals. We have a chance to make a difference, to influence policy development and importantly to work with government, our departmental colleagues, industry and community to develop policies and implement programs for the betterment of the Australian community. That's an incredibly fortunate position to be in. It is an opportunity to build quality organisations, to develop and make effective policy, and to help drive and influence change."

Taylor is well placed to judge the performance of the Canberra bureaucracy. As a former state department head, and as a family man who commutes from Melbourne, he has had plenty of opportunity to get feedback from the outside on how the Federal service delivers. With both his children grown up, and a wife who is a professional in her own right, he goes home on most Friday nights and returns to Canberra on Sunday night, or Monday morning in summer when he can be sure the airport will not be fog-bound.

So does he think the Canberra bureaucracy is in touch with the rest of Australia? "I think Canberra is less remote today than it's ever been. Theoretically, any capital in a federal system can be remote. However, one of the great features of Canberra culture is a very strong understanding in the Australian Public Service that we are serving the Australian public and the Australian community. It is my observation that the public service does an extremely good job to listen and understand the issues across the extraordinarily diverse range of communities that exist in our country. It's very easy for people to say Canberra's remote. But I could just about think of any town or capital city in Australia that you could describe as equally remote from the breadth of experience."

The portfolio of Transport and Regional Services should give Taylor plenty of opportunity to consider many Australian perspectives, but a task each department head has been given, to take a personal interest in a small number of specific indigenous communities, adds to the potential insight. "I'm involved in working with four indigenous communities in the East Kimberley region," he says. "East Kimberley sounds pretty good until you realise that it means the Tanami desert, near the WA and NT border." He goes there about three times a year to work with his West Australian government counterpart and the East Kimberley community to help implement changes to lift the well being of the communities. This is part of the "joined up government" that is much talked about today – and an approach to end petty bureaucratic fights and achieve real results.

Taylor grew up in urban and rural Victoria. His grandparents were farmers and his father an accountant. He spent time in the wheat sheep belt region of North West Victoria which he describes as "seriously challenging country". He regards the first 20 year mix of urban and bush life when he was growing up as a "huge plus". "The mix of urban upbringing in Melbourne, matched by a farm and regional upbringing gave me many insights that are indelibly etched in my mind even to this day about life's challenges," he says. "When you spend a fair bit of your early life growing up in a farmhouse without power, running your lighting on Shellite, having three taps – a hot and a cold one or dam water, and another tap that you drink on, a kero fridge, no inside toilets, but you have a fantastic, hard working farming and community environment."

Taylor said that gave him his passion for working with communities. "I have always had a huge interest in science, which I think a lot of us had in the early 60s when we were growing up. However, probably what really challenged me most, when I first started going to University, was starting to come to grips with the breadth of economic policy issues."

Taylor completed an Agricultural Science degree at Melbourne University and then added a Diploma in Economics at the University of New England. He has been an on-going economics student ever since, saying that it is through economics that we've been able to handle a lot of the really tough social and environmental issues. The economic reforms, particularly in the agricultural, natural resource and water management issues in which he has spent a lot of his life, have, he says, made a huge difference to the well-being of Australians.

Initially Taylor worked in the Victorian Department of Agriculture. There were many important policy changes around agriculture research, marketing reform and trade in the 70s and 80s; and, with his economics, he found a lot of opportunities. "I take pride in being involved in working with industries, particularly on reform issues, where you're deregulating things, but successfully achieving reform with industry ultimately in agreement."

Taylor got to see the reforms from both sides of the fence doing a stint with the Australian dairy industry, driving their international and national market reform program for about two years. He then went back to head the Victorian Department of Agriculture in the early 1990s, when the Victorian public service went through major productivity improvements. This period included difficult years of downsizing that saw public service numbers fall by about one third, to 100,000. "In my own department, there were many positive developments and changes. However, these downsizing changes were particularly difficult. These were people I knew well so you can imagine the personal grief when you are involved in making those reductions," he says.

"[W]e worked incredibly hard with all the people who were leaving the organisation, as well as those who were staying ... it was one of the most emotional periods I've ever been through in my life." Both he and those who were leaving ended up in tears. "You can't go through this process with not feeling it. You can even tell, I still feel it ... the really nice thing in hindsight is discovering how many people subsequently said that this was ultimately a good change even though it wasn't good at the time." Taylor says the people he works with are fundamental to driving success and "it doesn't matter whether you have a situation where you are changing or building, you have to treat people positively in exactly the same genuinely caring sense".

After heading up other Victorian departments, Taylor was invited to come to Canberra to head the Agriculture, Fisheries and Forestry department in 2000. He had been working on Commonwealth/state relations most of his working life; in agricultural, water and natural resource management and he knew many of the people he was to work with in Canberra. The time suited him. His two daughters were either at, or about to go to, university.

Taylor has the reputation for working long hours, often fuelled by copious amounts of caffeine. "I always enjoy getting up early," he says. "I'm always here before 7 o'clock and that's a great time. You get a lot of things done before everyone else arrives. My job ends when I go to bed, which is some time late at night – because I usually spend some of the evening meeting with colleagues, community or industry groups. He says in the course of a working week it wouldn't matter where he was living, he would not get much time with his family. But are these long working hours commendable or an example of poor delegation? Taylor laughs at this question. "Look, I wouldn't get anything done around this place without my colleagues, I can assure you. Delegation in this job is fundamental."

He says an important part of his working week is thinking – about both the people, the short, medium and long term policy and delivery requirements, and organisational management. "An important part of the day for me is the early morning – my planning and thinking time. During the day I'm delegating and working with my colleagues here, or working with either industry, or state or international colleagues, implementing the breadth of the policy and operational programs of our organisation."

Evenings are spent either talking with colleagues from the states or industry about broad policy issues, such as how to drive rail reform, or move on roads. "That is an issue. That really high level thing that you can't actually delegate. It's something you've got to make a choice about. Do you do that during the day, and put a lot of time in that day and not provide time for your colleagues? Or do you do that at night, when your colleagues quite rightly are spending time with their families? I'm a great believer in balance, so I know you're quite rightly saying, have you guys got it right? That an important choice I've made. I'm being honest about that."

"Despite my own behaviour, I am a great believer in balance and I constantly challenge my colleagues about spending time with their family and friends."

This article was first published in the Canberra Times on 20 March 2006

Pioneering Survivor – Helen Williams, Department of Communications, Information Technology and the Arts

As head of the Public Service Board some twenty-five years ago, Bill Cole told a tale of a senior officer in his former Finance department threatening that a woman would be appointed to the second division "over his dead body". Cole said he appointed the woman, but the senior officer did not die. The woman in question was Helen Williams, now head of the Department of Communications, Information Technology and the Arts.

Williams says there was "a bit of tension" back in 1979 when she joined the second division in Finance. There had been one woman second division officer in Treasury, but she was the first in Finance. She was well aware, in particular, of the opposition from the division head who went on to make Williams' life extremely difficult. "In those days, if you wanted increased staff you had to put a case to the Public Service Board," she says. "I was in charge of the social security branch and I think I had about five or six staff and I put up a case for an increase. I found out, when my division head was away, and there had been no response from the Board, that he'd actually told the Board not to take any notice it. I sent them a separate case and got the additional staff."

"At another stage he told me to fill in daily sheets showing what work had been done and the time I had spent on it." Williams filled out the reports until she bumped into the then head of her department, Ian Castles, at a departmental happy hour. "He asked me what the sheets were and, when I explained, said simply, 'why do you do it?'. I went to see the division head and said, 'Look, this is silly. It's a waste of my time', and the process was quietly dropped." Williams said she had not thought of going to Castles, or one of the deputies, to talk about it. "I tended to grit my teeth and think I will last this out. I learned through that experience."

Williams has been in the top rank of the public service for twenty years now. Before Peter Shergold, the current head of the Department of the Prime Minister and Cabinet, had even joined the public service, Williams was a department head. She joined the service in 1970 under the old Public Service Board administrative trainee scheme. Both her parents were academics, her father, Sir Bruce Williams, was Vice Chancellor of Sydney University and her mother, Roma Williams, had lectured in economics.

"I started to do a further degree and realised this wasn't going to be my future," she says. "I didn't like lecturing. I'm still not a good public speaker. And I decided to come to the public service to give myself a year to think about what

I really wanted to do." In her first year she had a major car accident and spent four months in Canberra Hospital. "I came out shaken and on crutches, and the Board decided to send me to Treasury as a place that required the least physical mobility." The car had crushed Williams, smashing both her legs, creating a condition known as a fat embolism where the bone marrow in her legs got into her blood stream and blocked the circulation to her lungs. "I was a write-off. I was very lucky there was a trauma team in Canberra Hospital that was researching ways to counter this kind of situation and they quite literally used me to experiment and brought me through."

Williams was in Treasury before it split into the two agencies of Treasury and Finance and she moved to Finance after the split. She worked mostly in the social security stream but also spent time on education and superannuation and rose to a level equivalent to the current Band Two. On the change of Government in 1983 she got a call from Dr Peter Wilenski who was the head of the Education department. He was a great supporter of women at senior levels of the service and asked Williams to apply for a deputy secretary position. "I think he was just increasing the number of women in the field," she says. "I don't think he, or I, expected me to get the job. But it's interesting to think back on how the representation of women has changed. Although the statutory authorities had more senior women, for example Marie Coleman was appointed head of the Social Welfare Commission in the early seventies, that was the first time a woman had reached a deputy secretary in a government department."

Williams says another example of the way things have changed is the attitude of the education community at the time to her appointment. "There was a real tension in the academic/education community about bringing somebody in from Treasury/Finance rather than an educationalist. Several articles were written at the time attacking the move." Even though Williams had a history/sociology background, the educationalists were very firmly of the view that she was a Treasury/Finance import. The economic rationalist debate had yet to gather steam, but she thinks there was an understanding that that was the way things were moving, and the educationalists did not like it. However, she says, it did not take long until she was accepted.

In 1985 she was appointed Secretary of Education. At that stage, she says the educational hierarchy in the states was very strong, particularly at the schools level. The state directors-general objected to any interference from the Commonwealth, or even from their own political leaders. "One of our tasks, in line with Labor's election policy, was to negotiate resource agreements for the general recurrent schools grants with both the states and the non-government systems. It was not easy because before that they got a free ride." Although the Commonwealth had the carrot of funding, the states had previously received the money without conditions. The Commonwealth Government now wanted a focus on its own priorities and some data on performance in meeting them as a condition of funding. Agreements were negotiated with the non-government systems, but the directors-general held out even though the priorities were not very different to those they already had.

Eventually the minister, Senator Susan Ryan, took the matter to the political level and achieved agreement. "I well remember the next Commonwealth-state officials meeting," Williams says. "I was given a very hard time because I'd allowed this to go to the political level when the directors-general had stated clearly that this wasn't going to happen ... in those days their firm view was that politicians should not interfere in their territory."

The Labor Government also moved the big funding programs for schools from the Schools Commission back to core government. Because the programs were very important to the Catholic systems, one or two of the Labor ministers were concerned about moving these programs into a department headed by a non-Catholic. It was the era of the campaign against state aid for independent schools and Williams says she was taken to Sydney to be vetted by the Catholic hierarchy. Although she had a Methodist background she got on extremely well with them and admired the Catholic school systems. "They were very efficient bureaucracies," she says.

Perhaps more surprising than the job discrimination and the religious concerns was the reaction to Secretary Williams' decision at the beginning of 1987 to take six months maternity leave. "That caused a considerable reaction both from the senior bureaucracy and from the women's groups," she says. "Both areas believed I'd let them down." Some of the women's groups believed she had been given a chance at a top job and should have either kept working or not had the baby. "I can understand their reaction," she says. "But it's one of those life choices you have to make."

While she was away, the head of the Department of the Prime Minister and Cabinet, Mike Codd, completed a reorganisation of the 28 departments, cutting them down to 18. "The day I came back from maternity leave was the day that the change was instituted and not surprisingly I was not one of those that got a department. I became one of the 10 or so Associate Secretaries." Williams was an associate secretary for five years. Half way through that period, Codd rang her and offered her the choice between running a particular agency and heading the secretariat of the Hawke Government's New Federalism exercise. "In my time in Education I'd seen at first hand the tensions and inefficiencies between the Commonwealth and the states and I was really attracted to the idea of trying to sort that out. So I chose the Hawke New Federalism exercise and I worked on that for the next three years."

The first Special Premiers' Conferences were a real success and there were some early gains. The particular group of premiers, led by the Premier of NSW, Nick

Greiner, wanted change and initially it looked as though that potential was going to be achieved. But the problem was funding. This was before the GST was brought in and the vertical fiscal imbalance between the Commonwealth and the states was the big issue. There was considerable concern at the Commonwealth level about giving up some of its funding power and Williams says this became a focus of the tensions between Hawke and Keating over the prime ministership. Ultimately the exercise stalled. But it remains an issue of real interest to her.

Williams says that one thing that has changed for the better over the years is the increased collegiality across the service and the positive encouragement to talk through issues of concern. " When I took over Education it had an extraordinarily low resource base … we really were fighting to achieve the change that was necessary. It didn't occur to me to talk to the head of PM&C about the problems we were facing or to make them more widely known. I think it's more generally accepted these days that, if you have a problem, you should talk to a senior manager."

She says all departments at some stage will have difficult inter-personal relationships. "I make it clear that I have an open door and people do come and talk to me about a range of problems, although I can understand some people are a bit hesitant to do so. But this is a general policy across the agency. I think the important thing is to make it clear that, if you have got a problem, there are systems to work the issue through." Williams does not favour moving people to overcome inter-personal problems in all but really difficult cases. "If there's a problem there's usually a way through it. It may be a case of insensitivity or unreal expectations on either side. It's important to work through the issues and consider possible solutions."

DCITA does not have a formal mobility scheme and Williams says "They can be too directive and I've suffered from these in the past myself. But I do positively encourage people to move to broaden their expertise." The other side of increasing mobility is the common complaint from outsiders that they never deal with the same public servant two weeks in a row. Williams says there is a line between being in a job long enough to have developed worthwhile experience and networks, and being there so long that one is stale. There are also ways of increasing experience through formal development activities or the addition of cross-agency responsibilities. "But I do believe that too frequent change is not good for an organisation. There is a real danger of losing essential expertise. I think that three or four, perhaps five, years is probably a good time in any one position. But often that depends on the particular person and the particular job. Some people go into a position with relevant experience and can hit the ground running. Others require time to develop new skills. But I don't believe, particularly at Secretary level, constant moves are helpful. It takes a while to get across the range of issues dealt with by a portfolio, particularly one where you've had no previous experience."

The public service has changed dramatically since Williams first became a secretary in 1985. Although she was personally disadvantaged by the major amalgamation of departments the Hawke Government implemented in 1987, she applauds the move. Williams, who was head of one of the existing 28 departments, Education, found herself sidelined as an associate secretary and had to work her way back to lead a full department again. By 1993 she was head of the boutique Department of Tourism and at the change of government was appointed to lead Immigration and Multicultural Affairs under minister Philip Ruddock.

There are few people today better placed to have observed the changes in the service over the last twenty years. Williams held key, central positions and took over the role of Public Service Commissioner in 1998, following Dr Peter Shergold, the current head of the Department of the Prime Minister and Cabinet. As Commissioner she was able to continue the reforms Shergold had started. In 1985 when there were 28 departments she says there were fewer linkages across government. "There were constant administrative orders changes and it really was a major problem for stability and efficiency. "You may remember the cartoons every time there was a change in government, or Prime Minister. Significant parts of departments used to pack up everything and move to a new agency. Since the 1987 amalgamations there have been minor changes to portfolios but they really have been remarkably stable since that time."

In 1985, she says, departments' policy advice was less contested. The growth in contestable sources of advice from think tanks, ministers' offices and consultants had not really taken off. In addition, the departments were less complex than today and central agency control, be it Finance or the Public Service Board, was "very much greater". As a result the management role of secretaries and their accountability was less significant. "If every time you wanted a change in departmental structures you had to go to the Public Service Board, you had less flexibility and less ability to be efficient and innovative," she says. "But you could also blame the Board if you didn't get what you believed you needed to do the job."

Finance and budgeting were also very different. "In those days you had to submit annual budget bids for each program item and had little ability to shift funds between program elements or years. So you didn't have the forward planning ability or the flexibility that you have today. The financial and personnel management changes since that time were driven by the public service itself, much of it under the aegis of the former Management Advisory Board."

In 1998, after having been Secretary of three departments and having headed the Commonwealth-State Relations Secretariat, Williams was appointed Public

Service Commissioner. "The main issue we faced was putting in place the new Public Service Act which represented a very major change in the way the departments were managed," she says. "Peter [Shergold] had done most of the ground work on the Act but we still had to negotiate it with the unions and support the minister, David Kemp, in negotiating it with the Opposition. David Kemp was really an ideal minister for that because he had a very good intellectual framework for the interaction between government and the public service. It was quite a long negotiation but eventually the Act was passed with bipartisan support."

"We went from an Act of about 300 pages full of very detailed prescriptions and regulations to an Act of about 45 pages which really just outlined the employment framework and set out the Public Service Values for the first time in legislation. It was based on devolution of power to agencies, but far greater accountability for the use of that power. In a way that's a far more difficult thing to manage than to operate within the safety of rules and regulations. But it also provided more flexibility, more potential for innovation and was a far more efficient system. It does put a lot more responsibility on the leaders of the service – and I'm talking here not only about secretaries but about people in the SES and even the executive levels of the service – to lead by example." She says the values were a careful balance between the need to be responsive to the Government-of-the-day and the apolitical professionalism of the public service.

Today, heading Communication, Information Technology and the Arts, Williams says she has "a fascinating portfolio". "I've enjoyed all my jobs but I have to say this one is particularly interesting, partly because of the diversity of the department. It has a broad range from the communications areas of telecommunications, broadcasting, ICT and the information economy, through to arts and culture and of course to sports."

In addition to the department, the portfolio has 21 other agencies. Williams says there is an increasing synergy across the tasks they undertake, starting with increasing convergence between the traditional communications areas of telecommunications, broadcasting and ICT which affects both regulation and market structures. For example, "you can now get the traditional broadcasting content on 3G mobile, or on computer via broadband. The old distinctions are increasingly obsolete and that impacts not only on policy advice but on the structure of the department. We're currently work-shopping ways to re-structure the department based on the more relevant divisions of content, carriage, and access."

The program load of the department has also increased significantly. DCITA is preparing to implement the $1.1 billion Connect Australia programs to increase communications in regional Australia in preparation for a possible final sale of Telstra. "That is a very major focus for the department next year. And, it's quite a test for us because the Government is focussing more and more on successful program implementation – getting results for the money it's putting into programs. The more expertise we can build in program management the more successful we will be. In fact increasing expertise generally is a core issue for all secretaries."

In the re-organisation, Williams plans to spread the programs across divisions to help build that expertise throughout the department. This will mean that coordinating mechanisms are particularly important to make sure that staff are aware of the overall picture. "The diversity of the areas we deal with, but also the synergies, mean that coordination across the department is a real priority," she says. "The important thing is to ensure that those mechanisms have their use-by date and don't go on after that date is reached."

On the synergies, she says that the growing importance of content to the future of communications generally means that the arts and culture side of the department is increasingly relevant to the communications side. This is particularly true of film and digital content. It is also relevant to sport as access to the various sports is obviously crucial to their financial position. "So the synergies are becoming more and more important in what seems at first to be a very diverse portfolio," she says.

Among the challenges Williams nominates for the department is the finalisation of the regulatory environment to give regulatory certainty for the Government's decision on the full sale of Telstra. "There are also some very big issues in the media field including the move to digital television and radio and the new triennium for the national broadcasters," she says. "In the sports area, we are in the closing stages of setting up the Australian Sports Anti-Doping Agency, and of course the Melbourne 2006 Commonwealth Games are now very close."

DCITA coordinates the Australian Government input into the Games. She says there are some major issues with the states over funding for the arts and culture. She gives as examples the sustainability of the orchestral sector and depreciation funding for the national collecting institutions, the Library, the Gallery, the Museum, and the Maritime Museum. Williams says the diversity is "part of the buzz" she gets from the portfolio.

The Secretary plays a key coordination role in the portfolio as well as the department. But unlike some department heads she does not have meetings of all 21 agency heads within the portfolio. "I don't think you would get senior people, say in Telstra, coming along on an ongoing basis to talk about arts funding," she says. But the heads of the cultural organisations do meet as a group and this group includes the ABC and SBS and the Australian Communications and Media Authority. "Every so often we also invite the sports agencies along to talk about particular issues. So we try and get as many of the portfolio agencies together as we can."

The meetings' agendas can range from specific funding or management issues to the contribution arts and culture can make to the economy and to the country's identity. "We also have regular meetings with the communications regulatory agencies, not only the Australian Communications and Media Authority, which is in this portfolio, but the Australian Competition and Consumer Commission."

Within the department, a regular weekly division heads meeting is held on Monday, exchanging information on what is happening in each of the areas, and considering management issues such as recruitment or occupational health and safety. There is also a monthly meeting of the executive group, consisting of Williams and her deputies, to discuss high-level issues arising for the department as a whole.

Contact with the ministers' offices is a priority. "One of our tasks is to ensure that there is an ongoing exchange of information so that the office and the department are aware of the other issues and concerns," she says. "That's immensely important." She observes that different ministers operate in different ways. "Some of them will pick up the phone whenever there's an issue. Others prefer face to face meetings. It will often depend on what the issues are."

It is also crucial to understand ministers' agendas to provide them with the best support. When a new government comes in, she says there is usually a well worked through policy platform. As governments are in power for any length of time, that agenda is revised and updated and the public service can provide very important assistance in that updating. "I can remember the then head of the British Cabinet Office telling me that when the Blair Government came in, it was extraordinarily impressed with the civil service because it had studied the Blair agenda, knew what to do to implement it and moved quickly to do so. Once that agenda needed revision, the Blair Government started to question why the process had stalled and the relationship started to falter. I think the lesson is that the Government and the public service must work together actively on policy development or the overall product suffers."

This article was first published in the Canberra Times on 6 February 2006

Taking the 'Hospital Pass' – Jane Halton, Department of Health and Ageing

Jane Halton ran into former Prime Minister Bob Hawke at a dinner reception for the Queen in Canberra. "Where did I first meet you?" Hawke asked. "Don't you remember?" For Halton it was a memorable experience. As a director in the Finance department and eight months pregnant she was summoned to attend an Expenditure Review Committee of the Cabinet. Historically, Finance officers have exposure to Cabinet processes at a more junior level than officers in other departments. When an item they are involved with is listed for consideration, they go and sit next to the Minister for Finance. "I think it was the first time that I went in this role and Hawke was in the room," Halton says. "The doors to the Cabinet room weigh an absolute tonne so there I was with about eight months worth of baby, first having to haul on these doors to try and open them, and then walking in. I was wearing a bright red dress. I can still remember Bob Hawke stubbing out his cigar in a sort of irritated action and just watching my stomach come up the room."

This was one of many such Cabinet experiences for Halton – not all of them pleasant. Finance, with its reputation for critically assessing ministerial proposals, often faced a hostile reception and Halton recalls the grillings. She says it was a good experience attending the meetings because they gave her an understanding of what government was concerned about. "You have to know your stuff and you learn not to be intimidated," she says. "I still remember an exchange with Graham Richardson [former Hawke-Keating minister] which had him sort of leaning out – he was on the same side of the table –and looking down the table and shouting at me with absolute intensity because something he had said was not right and we'd been obliged to point it out."

Did these experiences make Halton tough? "I think you had to have a confidence about what you did and didn't know," she says. "It made me very aware that you had to be clear of the facts to the greatest extent possible ... with Cabinet, if you didn't know, you had to say, 'I don't know' because the one thing you could never do was mislead people. And if you did mislead people you had to go back and correct, very quickly. Did it toughen you up? I think it does actually." Halton then adds that there is no second chance in making a case. The best case had to be put in the first instance.

Language in these exchanges can be fairly robust but Halton recalls that her first finance minister, Peter Walsh was from the old school. "I remember the first time I went up to Walshie's office, sitting in the ante room and I could hear this stream of language. Every word you can think of was being conjuncted with every other. Really his facility for use of the four letter word was truly amazing. And I can remember the door opening and somebody saying, 'Ah. Minister I'd like you to meet Jane Halton' and I walked in and we then had this very robust conversation about something which he was quite cranky about. He did not use one improper word, not even one modest, almost swear word. Nothing. So as soon as I walked in the room the language improved." She says Walsh was excellent to work with and had very strong views. "He had a couple of particular passions where I think he could go from idiosyncrasy to one-eyed. But he was very open to a debate and you could put to him the facts and have the argument with him."

The experience with Walsh may have been good training for Halton who would find herself 15 years later working as deputy secretary under Max-the-axe – Max Moore-Wilton, the head of the Department of the Prime Minister and Cabinet. "Max is a character," Halton says. "I actually very much enjoyed working with Max. People used to say to me, 'Don't you find Max scary? Don't you find him difficult?' because Max has a formidable intellect and he's very quick.' And I say to people who ask, 'No. Not compared to my father,' because that kind of quick intellect and that kind of quick intellectual debate is something we had at the dinner table and that style was very familiar to me. So Max and I always got on very well." Halton says if she had a point of view she found that she could always argue the case with Moore-Wilton and if she had a factual base or a good argument, he would shift his position. "But you had to be able to argue your case," she says.

It was in her period as Deputy Secretary of PM&C that Halton hit the headlines over her role as convener of the People Smuggling Taskforce in the Children Overboard Affair. What happened has been the subject of parliamentary examination and is now a matter of public record. In brief, Halton says that while she was chairing a meeting of the Taskforce a call came in from a senior defence member on that committee saying that children had been thrown overboard from an asylum seekers' boat known as SIEV 4. "I took that call and I relayed that back to the meeting," she says. "What I didn't know was that one of the other people in that meeting actually pushed back from the table and told Minister Ruddock [the Immigration minister] about what had just been relayed to us … I didn't know that," she says. The next day the issue was front page news.

Halton says that, "when we read things in the media we don't necessarily know where it's come from … Now it's a matter of record that there was a brief that was provided to Government which included that statement [that children had been thrown overboard] which was cleared by senior defence people as being accurate. And the reasons why the facts did not become clear until much later and the record corrected, are also a matter of record." She says she has learnt from this experience that, "first, it's very difficult when you're working under a great deal of time pressure – which this was – to actually sit and consider what appeared at the time minor or peripheral snippets of information and understand their implications. When things were moving incredibly quickly it needed someone to step up and say very clearly, 'We think there's a problem with that'. The facts of the matter which may be perfectly clear with hindsight, may not be at all clear at the time."

She adds that there are also crucial lessons for record keeping, which she impresses on her department. She says the question of who is responsible in a committee, or taskforce situation, is an interesting one. "Essentially, and one of the things I said in my evidence, was that the committee was not a decision making body. It wasn't. It was an information sharing body and it was a way of collating information and providing that information in a coherent fashion. But it did not supplant the role of the individual agencies."

By way of example in her portfolio she says the Department of Health and Ageing is working in a whole-of-government way on petrol sniffing. "Police, health services, employment services, family and community services and across state and federal boundaries are all needed to tackle this problem ... We have got everyone in this tent, which is right and proper. But at the end of the day, whose responsibility is addiction? Mine! And I know that. So I'm very conscious that we in this department don't try and shift our core responsibility on these sorts of issues." On the ground on any particular day others, such as the police, have to deal with the situation. Halton says, for example, that if there are bylaws that prohibit trafficking in fuel in a community where the non-sniffable petrol, Opal, had been introduced it would be the job of the local police to enforce the law. Her department, on the other hand, was dealing with the issue of the availability of Opal.

"While the Australian Government has made a huge commitment to the rollout of Opal fuel, we are actually constrained by the production capacity of the fuel company," she says. All the communities that had asked for Opal had got it but its introduction is not that simple. "If you want to put Opal in a roadhouse and Opal is made by one company and the roadhouse uses another company, what are you going to do about the fuel card that people bring in to that station? You've got to work through all those sorts of issues. It's not that simple." The department was working through these issues one by one.

Despite her experience in the Children Overboard affair, Halton remains a strong supporter of the system of parliamentary scrutiny. "I have a strong view that we have an incredibly robust democracy and public service," she says. "We have an incorrupt public service ... this department is very open to scrutiny. I don't object to the scrutiny we get from committees." She says she has discussed this issue with some of those who grilled her over Children Overboard and expressed her support for the process. "That said, it's not a personally pleasant thing to go through," she says. "One of the most difficult things in the public service is being a public face, because we don't seek the limelight. That's not why we do these jobs. If I wanted to be a public face, I would not be a public servant." Being in the limelight is an uncharacteristic role, and being a public servant leaves no right of response. "You don't comment." The limelight also had an impact on her family as journalists staked out her house at a time when her boys were 12 and 8 years old.

Halton may be the nearest thing we have to superwoman. On the morning of her first day as head of the Health in January 2002, she led an aerobics class at Deakin Health spa. At that time, the mother of two was at the centre of the Children Overboard inquiry, the hottest media and parliamentary story of the day. Her cross examination continued for months after she took over at Health. As if heading up a department was not enough, Halton still cooked her family's nightly meals and prepared lunches for her two boys, now aged 16 and 12. The affair gave Halton a public profile that public servants generally seek to avoid and saw her described as "tart", "forceful", "hardworking" and "combative."

Today running the Health department, Halton says her department's challenge is to maintain the good health that the vast majority of Australians enjoy. "Our fundamental challenge is to work on a system that delivers great outcomes for all Australians … we've got to make sure that we maintain that position. We have a good health system, we get it at a reasonable cost on any comparison … we have great science, research, great access to world leading technology … Our challenges are to maintain that position, make sure of our funding arrangements and continue access to practitioner services, particularly in rural and remote areas … It's also important to tackle the problems we have with people who don't have the same level of outcomes – indigenous people are the clearest example."

Halton says there is a real passion inside the department about tackling issues of indigenous health. Our challenges for the future include major reforms in mental health and the ongoing developments in electronic health. This includes the development of technology that means people do not have to repeat all their details every time they go and see a medical practitioner. "What happens if you get run over by a bus in Bourke Street in Melbourne and the hospital doesn't know who you are and you are incapable of telling them? How do we get your medical records quickly in that sort of emergency situation? Do they know that you might be allergic to penicillin or something else? "

Regional responsibilities are also taken seriously with the department contributing expertise and funding for health services in the South Pacific and the Asia Pacific region. Helping to build the capacity of the region to handle the threats of such things as avian influenza and HIV/AIDS will help both the region and Australia. The big issue is the possible avian influenza pandemic where the department must make sure that Australia is well positioned against something which is uncertain and relatively unknown. "I am delighted that we are recognised as world leaders in our pandemic preparedness and response plans," Halton says. "I'm told that regularly by the head of the WHO and by people who come out of the UN in New York."

She also draws attention to the potential threat of a terrorist attack using biological agents, for which the department is well prepared. On ageing issues she says she was really pleased when the Treasurer took the issue up because it had been a boutique issue – something Health worried about and the pensions people worried about because they could see the bill mounting. But with the demographic change inevitable, Australia needed to think about the issue. There was a need to improve productivity and participation, and provide quality and flexible services for the future.

There is no doubt Halton is tough. You have to be a woman who has risen to head a department at age 42 – the youngest head in the service at that time. Halton came to Canberra as a 13 year old in 1973, when her father was appointed head of the Department of Transport. Her father, a United Kingdom industrialist, had taken his family to Canada in 1969, where he worked as a bureaucrat for almost five years. Halton's early years were spent living in a farmer's cottage outside a tiny village called Rangeworthy. "As a small child I lived in a very rural environment in a tiny cottage," she says. "You had to walk up a very long lane, even to get to the main road and then you could walk into the village where I went to school." The small two room primary school had a series of tables where children of similar ages gathered and where Halton learnt to read and write.

Halton's father worked in aviation on projects like the Bloodhound rocket. One of her early memories is sneaking into the factory underneath a blanket on the floor of the back of the car to see the Concorde aircraft's nose going up and down. Canberra was a big adventure. The family moved into Hughes and Halton went to Deakin High School. "That was a terrible shock to the system because I had to wear a school uniform and I'd avoided school uniforms in my earlier academic career." Halton says she was "appalled" because the summer uniform was a "disgrace" and the winter uniform was "ghastly". "I just refused to wear it … I wore summer uniform the whole time, just with a jumper over the top. I was extremely stubborn." When teachers suggested she might be cold she responded that, "compared with Canada this is quite warm thank-you very much".

Halton went on to Phillip College and today finds that her oldest son, who has just gone to Narrabundah, is being taught by a couple of teachers who actually taught her and her husband. (Uniform rebelling runs in the family. Her oldest son almost steadfastly refused to wear a uniform through his high school career. Halton says she "had a little sympathy for him"). At college Halton was on the debating team and was also keen on sport. As a child she had danced a lot and in Canada she took up skating and skiing. When she went to university she played volleyball and squash. For 20 years, up until her first day as head of the Department of Health she had taught aerobics. When she is in Canberra Halton tends to get to work at about 9 am, unless she has an early meeting. Often she does not go home until 7.30 pm. "We eat late," she says. "I would tend to cook while they're home and we try to convene the family over the dinner table." To the suggestion that she is performing a 1950s conventional housewife role as well as heading a department she says, "No, you misunderstand the role my husband plays in all this. He generally takes half, or more than half of the load. But I like cooking."

Halton toyed with doing a number of things at university but ended up doing a double major honours degree in psychology. On graduation she went to the Australian Bureau of Statistics for a short period but then got a job as a research assistant in the Research School of Social Sciences working on Ageing and Family. It was work in an area which has now become a career interest. She considered becoming an academic but decided it wasn't for her because "there probably wasn't enough adrenalin in it ... You've got to recognise what you're like and what you're good at and I just decided that it didn't have the pace that I liked," she says. "So I thought if it doesn't have the pace that I want, what I might do is start work in the public service for a while and I'll think what I'll do when I grow up."

She went back to the Bureau of Statistics and worked on labour market statistics, giving her an appreciation of the market issues. She also worked on the Special Supplementary Survey looking at families. While debating what to do next she applied for various jobs and got a Clerk Class 7 in the ABS, a considerable leap. The next day she was also offered a Clerk Class 6 in the Aged Person Welfare Branch in the Department of Social Security. She consulted a senior colleague who told her, "You can come back to the ABS any time. Go and try out there in the policy world ... That was very good advice," she says. There she worked, among other things, on the Home and Community Care program, which paradoxically, she came back to run years later.

She then went to work on Medicare and the Health Care Agreements. "That was very good because that showed you how government manages inter-government relationships," she says. "It also showed you how government managed the financial relationships between levels of government and it introduced you to the complexity of things like the Grants Commission ... Things were not necessarily as they seemed – the drivers, and incentives, understanding that complexity again has proved incredibly useful during my career."

Having done that Halton thought it would be a good long term career move to transfer to the Department of Finance. "I was being told effectively, just hang round for a bit and you'll be an SES officer. And I made a conscious decision that I didn't need to be an SES officer before I was 30," she says. "Basically ... one of the things I had learnt early was that breadth of experience and perspective are incredibly important and secondly, you need to understand the different players in any part of the environment in which you work ... One of the great advantages I had in the Community Care Program is working with a lot of people in the community sector, understanding the consumer issues, understanding what were the drivers and what were the challenges that some of these people faced in their day to day lives. To be able to bring back the experience and perspective to bear upon the policy perspective is incredibly useful ... I then realised that I needed to understand more about the things I had seen in the Medicare negotiations, about ... the issues around the money debates, what were the issues around the inter-governmental relationship issues? What were the things that led government in the centre to make decisions?"

Halton says running a department is like running a big business. Policy is her real interest but she thinks there is a much better chance of delivery on policy objectives if the department is well run. So she spent some time on her rise to the top gaining corporate experience, running the corporate services in the Health department. In Finance Halton had been one of a small number of women. Helen Williams had pioneered as the first Finance Senior Executive Service woman but had left by the time Halton arrived. Halton did two years there and had her first child while in Finance. She recalls sitting in Parliament House on the orange sofas and Brian Howe who was then a senior cabinet minister coming over and chatting to people from various departments. "He wandered over to me and he stood in front of me so I had to kind of lever myself to my feet and he said, 'We haven't met ... You're Charles' daughter'."

"I was petrified. Absolutely mortified, because the entire room just stopped. Every senior person in that room was listening and we then had a conversation about my dad ... It was very nice of him because he was coming over to say hello ... But I had always stayed away from the bits of the service where my father worked ... on the grounds that it was much better to stay away from his area of influence and people could never make a comment about unnecessary advantage, or coaching, or any of those other things. So there was this senior Cabinet minister acknowledging my parentage. My father was his first Secretary – they went way back."

Halton left Finance on promotion to come back to the Department of Health as an SES officer. She had her exit interview with Steve Sedgwick who later became

Secretary. By this stage, Finance had worked out that they should be sensitive about people, particularly women, and, when Sedgwick asked why she was going, she replied, "because I'm being promoted, Steve".

This article was first published in the Canberra Times on 10 April 2006

www.ingramcontent.com/pod-product-compliance
Lightning Source LLC
Chambersburg PA
CBHW061240270326
41927CB00035B/3459